Engulfed in War
Just War and the Persian Gulf

Maluna a' e o nā lāhui apau ke ola ke kanaka
"Above all nations is humanity"

The Spark M. Matsunaga Institute for Peace of the
University of Hawai'i is an academic community
designed to develop and share knowledge about the root
causes of violence, the conditions of peace, and the use
of nonviolent means for resolving conflicts. Founded in
1985, the institute operates with openness to all views
and with a commitment to academic freedom and rigor.
It is committed to improving education in peace studies
for graduate, undergraduate, secondary, and primary
school students; undertaking peace research to promote
understanding of issues of violence, nonviolence, social
justice, ecological vitality, freedom, and human dignity;
participating with community groups to communicate
with all segments of society on these issues; and publish-
ing scholarly and creative works on peace in all media.

Engulfed in War:
Just War and
the Persian Gulf

Edited by
BRIEN HALLETT

Spark M. Matsunaga Institute for Peace
University of Hawai'i
Honolulu, Hawai'i
1991

Engulfed in War : Just War and the Persian Gulf /
edited by Brien Hallett
     p.   cm.
Includes bibliographical references and index.
ISBN 1-880309-02-5 : $5.00
1. Persian Gulf War, 1991--Moral and ethical aspects
2. Just war doctrine. I. Hallett, Brien
DS79.72.E54 1991
956.704'3--dc20   91-39620
                                         CIP

CONTENTS

PREFACE

LIKE THE WAR ITSELF, this collection of essays was unexpected. No editor planned it. Unlike the war, the results are much happier and more positive. All can benefit by struggling with the large and daunting problems raised in these pages.

First, there is the question of the morality of war in general. Even if it were once possible to talk of a "just" war, is it still possible? And if so, how and why? What is the role, if any, of international law in assuring the justice of our wars? Second, there is the specific case of the Persian Gulf War: Was the response to Saddam Hussein's conquest of Kuwait just or unjust? Third, there is the future to consider: Have the just war criteria demonstrated-- once again--how vacuous they are? How they are an empty word game that politicians play to justify the unjustifiable, thereby distracting from their own failings to resolve the root causes of the war?

The questions are challenging, and the authors of these five essays defend their side of each controversy with vigor. Point and counterpoint, therefore, is the hallmark of this collection. This balanced, almost symmetrical, presentation was not, as I noted, planned. The first essay to arrive, in December 1990, was George Lakoff's "Metaphors and War," which is a brilliant deconstruction of the language used to talk about the Persian Gulf War, in particular, and the Fairy Tale of the Just War, in general. Then Donald Wells sent us "Can Modern Wars Be Just?" in January and Roger Williamson delivered "Engulfed in War" at a February 1991 Institute for Peace colloquium. Having received the stimuli, the responses could not be long in coming.

In the audience at Williamson's presentation was Meredith Kilgore, who took exception to Williamson's conclusion that a resumption of combat in Kuwait would not be justified. Energized by the colloquium and building upon work he was already doing, he wrote a rebuttal. In addition to giving a copy to us, he also submitted his essay to the Elie Wiesel Foundation for their Elie Wiesel Prize in Ethics contest and won second prize. We are most grateful to the Elie Wiesel Foundation for permission to include a revised version of the essay in this volume.

The response to Donald Wells's article, which is distilled from his book *War Crimes and Laws of War,* was principally mine.

While I agreed that the laws of war were derived both historically and logically from the just war criteria, I also felt that Professor Wells had slighted the criteria and that the shortcomings of international law resulted from defects in the international community and its institutions, not from defects in the just war criteria. In short, I felt that a reconsideration of the just war criteria was needed for balance.

All the essays thus were originally written in the months between November 1990 and February 1991. Rather than allow the authors the historical luxury of going back and reworking their essays in the light of subsequent events, they were instead invited to append postscripts reflecting on their earlier thoughts and the course of events in the gulf. These essays thereby provide examples of the best use of the just war criteria: impassioned minds grappling with, as Lakoff points out, literally vital issues from amidst the storm and confusion of ongoing events.

Stimulus and response, point and counterpoint. Thus it was that the five essays included in this study came together. No one had planned it that way, but the results are a serious and balanced look at some of the more difficult dilemmas that face us all. None of the authors pretends to possess all of the answers. Each, however, hopes that the confrontation of opposing views will assist the reader in clarifying his or her own thinking on these important and perplexing issues.

Brien Hallett
Honolulu
September 1991

Part I

The Tradition

War and conquest are a sad necessity in the eyes of men of principle, yet it would be still more unfortunate if wrongdoers should dominate good men.

St. Augustine

Any act of war aimed indiscriminately at the destruction of entire cities or of entire areas along with their entire population is a crime against God and man himself.

Second Vatican Council

The Just War Criteria: A Reconsideration

BRIEN HALLETT

Violence is by nature instrumental; like all means, it always stands in need of guidance and justification through the ends it pursues.
Hannah Arendt, *On Violence* (p. 150)

1. The Presuppositions

When one begins thinking about war many difficult questions come to mind--questions of terrain, command, and doctrine, of politics and economics, of life and death, and many more. However, the two most important questions are the definitional question, "What is war?" and the moral question, "Is this war just or unjust?"

The two questions are of course intimately related; the possibility of even asking the moral question depends upon the answer given to the definitional question. That is, if war be an unspeakably depraved tale of killing, maiming, and loved ones returning home in body bags, then war, like rape, can never be justified. It is always immoral and to even raise the moral question is the purest nonsense. However, if war be something other than the destruction of the enemy--a matter of policy, perhaps, as Clausewitz's dialectic argues--then the next logical step is to raise the moral question and ask whether or not this specific war can be justified.

A full account of the just war criteria, therefore, should begin by arguing that war is not the destruction of the enemy, that it possesses other means and purposes. Unfortunately space does not permit making that argument here. All that can be done is to note in passing that any discussion of the morality of specific wars presupposes that war itself is a human activity--like automobile driving or coal mining--that can be justified despite the enormous numbers of people killed and maimed as a result of the activity.

3

Having made my presuppositions explicit, the next difficulty in discussing the just war criteria is that very few people have ever read them. Very few people even know what they look like. To remedy this, two variants of the criteria are listed in section 2, immediately followed by a summary explanation of each criterion to indicate its general scope and intent. Following these explanations, my reconsideration of the just war criteria begins in earnest by attempting to come to grips with two issues. First, I will explain why the criteria have been held in such contempt for the last four hundred years, and second, I will disassociate the criteria from religion in general and Christianity in particular, establishing them upon purely secular foundations. The leitmotiv that weaves its way through both discussions is that, fortunately or unfortunately, there exists no alterative to the just war criteria--except silence. If one wishes to debate the justice or injustice of specific wars, if one wishes to come to well-considered judgments through reasoned debate, then there is simply no alternative to the just war criteria, our contempt and misunderstanding of them notwithstanding.

2. The Criteria

VERSION 1

A. Just Causes to Resort to War.
    1. To protect the innocent from unjust attack.
    2. To restore rights wrongfully denied.
    3. To reestablish an order necessary for a decent human existence.

B. Criteria for Determining a Just Cause:
    1. Lawful authority
    2. Clear declaration of causes and aims
    3. Just intention
    4. Last resort
    5. Probability of success
    6. Proportionality of ends
    7. Maintenance of justice in war
        a. Noncombatant immunity (Potter 1970)

VERSION 2

I. *Ius Ad Bellum* (Justice *To* War)
   A. Just cause against a real and certain danger
   B. Competent authority
   C. Comparative justice
   D. Right intention
   E. Last resort
   F. Probability of success
   G. Proportionality of ends

II. *Ius In Bello* (Justice *In* War)
   A. Proportionality of means
   B. Discrimination, namely, noncombatant immunity
   (National Conference of Catholic Bishops 1983)

Expanding upon the second version, the general scope of each criterion is as follows.

I. *IUS AD BELLUM (ACTIONEM)*

1) *Just Cause:* The traditional causes listed by Potter establish the general categories. For a more detailed analysis, one must turn to Aristotle's principle of double effect. That is, since every action produces both good and bad effects, the reasons for acting in a certain way in a specific case must be just. For example, sticking a knife in someone's chest is justified when the assailant is a surgeon seeking to repair the patient's heart, but unjustified when the assailant is a mafioso seeking to silence an informer.

2) *Competent (Legitimate or Lawful) Authority:* This is first and foremost a prohibition against private war. War is the *ultima ratio regum,* the ultimate reason of kings. Hence, only legitimate sovereigns may denounce war. The need for competent authority makes guerrilla wars or wars of national liberation extremely difficult to justify, since the guerrillas usually have great difficulty establishing their legitimacy. In addition, not only must the authority be competent in the general sense of being a legitimate sovereign, it (or its ally) must also be competent in the particular sense of being the legitimate sovereign over the territory under dispute in the war. And finally those who argue for or against the war, those who make the final decision, and those who wage the war must all be the proper people to do each of these tasks (Cicero's

constitutio translativa). In particular, the lawful authority of those who wage the war is essential if noncombatant immunity is to be maintained (compare with section II *ius in bello* below).

3) *Comparative Justice:* In general, the justice of one's cause must be sufficiently greater than the adversary's to override the presumption against war.

4) *Right Intention:* In general, this involves warring only for a just cause, and during the war avoiding unnecessarily destructive acts, unreasonable conditions such as unconditional surrender, and always seeking the first opportunity for reconciliation. In greater detail, despite the fact that the warring parties know their actions will produce unintended evil consequences, their own intentions must be good. For example, the surgeon, when amputating a leg, cannot do so if his primary intention is to cripple the patient for life.

5) *Last Resort:* Again since every action produces both favorable and unfavorable results, the most drastic option should be chosen only as a last resort. Thus, the intended results of the war must be judged in relation to, one, the accumulating injustice if nothing is done; two, the delayed arrival of justice if other less decisive options are chosen; and three, the unintended harmful consequences, both known and unknown, of the war. This criterion is particularly open to abuse. Some will use it as an excuse for never going to war, arguing that with just a little more time, negotiations or sanctions or whatever will succeed. Others, seeking an excuse for war, will make unreasonable demands and attack when these are not immediately accepted. Neither extreme captures the intent of the criterion.

6) *Probability of Success:* This criterion is primarily an injunction against lost causes. The "Masada Complex" leads far too often to unjust wars. Beyond prohibiting lost causes, proper interpretation of this criterion requires that one avoid the greater evil that will result from failure in war.

7) *Proportionality of Ends:* The good to be realized must be greater than the evil inflicted. In a world of limited resources and limited effects, the ends never justify the means. Only a relatively few actions can be justified as proportional to and compatible with the ends sought.

II. *IUS IN BELLO (ACTIONE)*

Having justified a decision to wage war, the debate is not finished. During the course of the war, the community must constantly monitor itself to ensure that the means selected do not negate the ends sought. Specifically the immunity of noncombatants from harm must be maintained. (Or in Pentagon jargon "collateral damage" must be minimized). This is achieved by means of two criteria:

1) *Discrimination of Means:* To maintain noncombatant immunity and to minimize the war's evil consequences and maximize its good consequences, only military facilities and persons will be attacked, and these will be attacked with the minimum amount of force required to achieve the objectives of the attack.

2) *Proportionality of Means:* To maintain noncombatant immunity, none of the acts of war may be so devastating as to render the whole war unjust by increasing the unintended evil and decreasing the intended good effects.

In other words, respect for noncombatant immunity means that the military principle of economy of force will be respected.

3. The Defamation of the Criteria

From even this brief commentary on the criteria, it should be clear that each and every one of them is debatable. Most frustrating of all, two people citing precisely the same facts will come to diametrically opposite conclusions, one saying that a war is just, the other that it is not. In the eyes of many, this is the greatest "defect" in the criteria. What good are a set of *just* war criteria, people ask, if they do not lead to clear-cut, firm decisions on the justice or injustice of a war?

Needless to say this "defect" makes the criteria exceptionally easy to ridicule, especially when they are mixed with religious pretensions. To name but two, Thomas More in his *Utopia* and Erasmus in numerous writings ridiculed just war thinking unmercifully. For example, in his colloquy *Charon,* Erasmus has Alastor relate to Charon, the ferryman over the River Styx:

> Certain creatures [the friars] . . . never leave the courts of princes. They [these friars] instill into their [the princes'] ears a love war; . . . they proclaim in their evangelical sermons that war is just, holy, and right. And--to make you marvel more at the audacity of the fellows--they proclaim the very same thing on both sides. . . . [And] none of those who die in a just war come to you [Charon], I believe. For these, they [the friars] say, fly straight to heaven. (Erasmus 1957, pp. 115, 117)

Erasmus, Thomas More, and others can hardly be blamed for satirizing the just war criteria when the uncertainty of the criteria allow "the friars" (and others) to claim justice for both sides. Moreover when such consummate cynics as Pope Julius II or Henry VIII loudly proclaim the justice of their wars, the result is a black comedy of the worst sort. But wherein lies the fault? Is it the criteria themselves, or the bad faith and insincerity of those who pervert the criteria for their own purposes? Clearly the latter. Are we to conclude that science and religion are ridiculous and irrelevant just because unscrupulous men have used them to justify slavery, genocide, and other crimes? It is the unscrupulous who must be ridiculed and condemned and rendered irrelevant, not science or religion. Likewise it is the cynics who must be condemned for any misuse of the just war criteria, not the criteria themselves. Nonetheless the ridicule heaped upon the criteria for four hundred years means that most people have dismissed them as laughable.

A second reason the just war criteria are held in such disrepute is that they are usually mislabeled. They are hardly ever called the just war *criteria;* instead they are usually called the just war *theory.* As a result, most people believe that the just war *theory* justifies war in general or in the abstract. *In general,* war can never be justified. To even begin to justify war *in the abstract* is an absurd task, an impossible task. It cannot be done. War quite simply is not a good in itself. War is too horrible and devastating to be justified *in the abstract* or *in general.*

What the just war *criteria* do, however, is to assist communities in choosing the lesser of two evils, not in the abstract, but in specific situations. When confronted with a concrete situation in which all options are unacceptable, the just war *criteria* analyze and compare the justice, the intentions, the ends, the probability of success, and so on between the opposing sides and among the options. They provide a disciplined structure in which all the relevant concerns can be debated and decided, in which the least unacceptable option may be identified. Sadly the lesser of the evils is sometimes war. But to say that war is the least unacceptable evil when Hitler has conquered all of Europe and is proceeding with the extermination of twelve million "undesirables" is not to say that war *in general* is ever justified. *In the abstract,* the just war criteria are meaningless. They become meaningful only when a concrete historical situation demands difficult choices among real alternatives. Then, and only then, is there something to debate. Then, and only then, do the just war criteria come alive as communities struggle to identify the lesser evil.

A third and related misconception is the view that the just war criteria are a mechanical device for determining the justice or injustice of a war. Like a mathematical formula, one plugs in the proper values, turns the crank, and grinds out the correct answer. There are two variations on this theme: a dictatorial assertion of personal bias and a servile search for an unfailing authority. The egotist, asserting his personal bias with finality, uses the criteria to proclaim a given war (or war in general) to be just or unjust precisely because he has determined it to be thus. End of discussion, period. In contrast, other less assertive personalities search for a supreme mathematician--a pope, a king, a president, a commissar--who will do all the hard work, who will compare the justice of each side, who will calculate the probability of success, who will measure the proportionality of means and ends and so on, and hand down indisputable answers.

Both variations, however, derive from a profound misunderstanding of the just war criteria, which are the very antithesis of a mechanical mathematical formula. By just looking at them, it should be evident that each criterion, not to mention the entire set, is infinitely debatable. There is never any certainty when debating the just war criteria. Never will there be an unfailing authority who can speak ex cathedra. Indeed, the entire purpose of the criteria is to provoke debate--a disciplined, organized debate to be sure; a difficult, anguished debate that all wish to avoid--but debate nonetheless. The presumption behind the just war criteria is not that there are clear-cut mechanical "answers" to difficult moral dilemmas, but rather that only reasoned debate allows communities to respond to the endless ambiguities of war with well-considered judgments.

In sum, for these and other reasons the just war criteria have been held in disrepute since the early sixteenth century, and as a result few people have ever actually seen them, much less taken them seriously. However, none of these reasons appears to be very substantial. They all seem to miss the point. Consequently, should the attempt not be made to rehabilitate the criteria?

4. Reconsidering the Just War Criteria

The biggest obstacle to any reevaluation of the just war criteria is war itself. To all appearances, wars are terrible and horrifying. They defy sanity, lacking the pretense of rhyme or reason or any sense of proportion in their seemingly senseless drive to kill, maim, and exterminate the enemy. Given this ghastly vista, how is one to think about the numerous wars that scar our history? Can one even *think* about war? Or are wars beyond thought, beyond reasoned debate, beyond well-considered judgments? Are our minds so paralyzed by their horrors that reasoned debate and well-considered judgments are not merely impossible but absurd as well?

I. HOLY WARS, PACIFISM, AND JUST WAR THINKING

The cultures of the world have responded to questions such as these with three conflicting attitudes or mentalities toward war: a holy war or crusade mentality, just war thinking, and pacifism. Of the numerous contradictions among these attitudes, the most important is between a holy war mentality and pacifism, on the one hand, and just war thinking, on the other. Both the crusader and the pacifist, although diametrically opposed, are absolutely certain about all aspects of war. Both already know the answers to any questions that one might have concerning a specific war.

This absolute certainty, and hence lack of debate, is in sharp contrast to the ambivalence and uncertainty of just war thinking, an ambivalence that is often ridiculed. Those who adopt a just war attitude are never sure; they are always debating the wisdom and justice of each war and of each action in each war. Indeed, coming to well-considered judgments by means of reasoned debate is precisely what the just war criteria are all about. A democratic faith in the ability of a people to reason their way to well-considered judgments, even in the most difficult and wrenching of circumstances, is the engine that drives the just war attitude. To abandon reason amidst the horrors of war, when it is most needed, is the ultimate horror that motivates the just war mentality. Consequently, from the point of view of just war thinking, both holy war and pacifism represent unacceptable extremes because both preclude well-considered judgments and reasoned debate.

Holy wars preclude such debate by appealing directly to divine authorities (or at least their earthbound spokesmen): "But of the cities of these people, which the Lord thy God doth give thee for an inheritance, thou shalt save alive nothing that breatheth: But thou shalt utterly destroy them; namely, the Hittites, and the Amorites . . . as the Lord thy God hath commanded thee" (Deut 20:16-17. But see Deut 9:5.) After receiving such unequivocal, such brutally clear instructions from the Deuteronomic authority, few would be so hardy as to question the justice of annihilating either the Hittites, the Amorites, or the other peoples condemned in the text.

Holy wars also suffer from two additional defects. First, they know no limits in their brutality. Annihilation is too good for the accursed of God. Second, when the forces of divine righteousness fail to win a clear-cut victory, the moral foundations of both the war and of the religious establishment itself are called into question. How, believers will begin to wonder, could a true God speaking through a truly holy man allow the righteous to suffer at the hands of the heretics and infidels?

In sum, a holy war mentality relieves the faithful of all moral responsibility, including the responsibility of thinking through the justice of the war. All their judgments are prepackaged; all debate has been rendered frivolous by 'the Lord thy God who hath commanded thee.' For those who feel the moral weight of their own actions, however, this mentality is difficult to accept.

Similarly pacifism precludes all debate by declaring all wars immoral a priori. Whether this specific war in these concrete circumstances can or cannot be justified is simply not a matter of concern for pacifists. Again the principal benefit of this attitude is moral certainty. Having ruled all wars unjust, the pacifist need not be troubled by thinking through the knotty moral dilemma of any specific, concrete war.

Pacifism also suffers from two additional defects. First, in its zealous effort to avoid sins of commission, it is willing to foster sins of omission. Certain that war is the ultimate evil, the pacifist is incapable of comparing war to any other evil, and hence is forced, without debate, to allow the other evil to continue indefinitely, so long as the supposedly incalculable evils of war are avoided. Second, whenever the dogs of war are let loose, the pacifist's silence is broken only to condemn the depredations of the war itself and the inattention to "root causes" that allowed the war to happen in the first place. That every war is "avoidable" if only its "root causes" had been attended to is tautologically true. Unfortunately though, such an approach is unhelpful in the extreme. The barn door is already open, the horse is already running free, and to suggest that the whole deplorable situation could have been avoided if only the door had been closed in the first place is more than a little irrelevant, its tautological truth notwithstanding.

In sum, for those who already possess certainty or for those who seek it, the defects of either a holy war or a pacifist mentality are but a small price to pay for eternal peace of mind. The prize is

great, the defects small.   For those, however, who are
uncomfortable with certitudes, for those who believe that neither
ecclesiastical authorities nor a self-evident "reality" relieve either
society or the individual from making reasoned judgments, the
radical uncertainty of just war thinking is not a defect. Indeed, it is
an invitation to wrestle with the infinite complexity of our world, to
debate with others, and finally to come to a well-considered
judgment together. For such people the open-ended inquiry that
characterizes just war thinking is the only possible approach to war.
Both holy war and pacifism are simply too closed and idealistic to
tempt such people. Unfortunately though, the sharp edge of the just
war criteria has been blunted by our inability to separate them from
their religious roots. Consequently an effort must be made to
disentangle the criteria from religion.

II. JUST WAR THINKING AND RELIGIOUS TRADITIONS

When not ridiculed or ignored, the just war criteria are usually
viewed as a quaint religious relic--something that depends upon
sacred scriptures for its moral authority, something that religious
leaders consult like tea leaves when making moral pronouncements
on war. The fact of the matter is that the just war criteria are
completely independent of religion, in general, and Christianity, in
particular.

Just war thinking is independent of Christianity because, as
already noted, practically every culture in the world possesses a just
war tradition. For example, certain passages in the *Iliad* articulate a
rudimentary set of just war criteria: "to fight for Helen and her
property (III, 70); "[to] take vengeance on men who break their
oaths" (III, 279), "injuring the host who entertained him" (iii, 353).
The entire *Bhagavad Gītā* is a long attempt by Vishnu to convince a
skeptical Prince Arjuna of the justice of fighting in the great battle
that is to be fought on the marrow. Sun Tzu in his *Art of War*
emphasizes that "moral influence" *[tao]* is the first factor to be
considered before engaging in war, a thought the commentator
Chang Yu elaborates as, "When troops are raised to chastise
transgressors, the temple council first considers the adequacy of the
rulers' benevolence" (Sun Tzu 1963, p. 63). And in republican
Rome one of the religious congregations, the *collegium fetiales,* was
responsible for sanctifying the ratification of treaties and declarations
of war in accordance with the *ius fetiale,* a well-established tradition
of law built upon the principle that "the only justification for war is

that peace and justice should afterwards prevail," as Cicero put it in *De Officiis* (1, ch. 11. Cf. Plato, *Laws* 628. Livy is the other principal source on the *collegium fetiales*. Vide Grotius 1925, pp. 633-39.) Clearly a mode of thinking found in all of the world's cultures cannot be the exclusive province of Christianity.

The just war criteria are likewise independent of all religion. The confusion here is historical. As a matter of history, all just war thinking in all cultures has developed within the context of religion. Religious thinkers have always been in the forefront of just war discussions. For example, John Calvin, with his Lesser Magistrates doctrine (*Institutes* 4, chap 20, no. 21), is the last innovative just war thinker in the European tradition. And religious leaders, as is their wont, always appeal to their gods. However, before our present secular age, no one found this strange. Where else would people go to seek solace, if not guidance, concerning war? War, like religion, engages our ultimate concerns; hence the natural context for discussing war has always been religion.

While certainly natural, it is not necessary. The just war criteria are easily developed without the slightest hint of religion.[1] There are basically two ways to do this: by appealing to natural law and the language of human rights, or by making an effort to work out the implications of Aristotle's principle of double effect. Since the sixteenth century international law has taken the first route. Breaking away from the canon lawyers, Grotius and his followers developed the laws of war and peace without an appeal to either religion or the gods, as a reading of the modern fruits of their labors, the Hague and Geneva conventions, will demonstrate.

More specifically, the two secular axioms from which the just war criteria follow are first, Cicero's previously cited dictum that "the only justification for war is that peace and justice should afterwards prevail" (cf. Grotius 1925, 770), and second, Grotius's conclusion that "[In ancient times] declarations of war . . . were wont to be made publicly [*ex dicto*], with a statement of the cause, in order that the whole human race as it were might judge of the justness of it" (Grotius 1925, 593). From Cicero's dictum it follows that war is not a mindlessly unbounded act of devastation, but a purposeful activity, limited in both ends and means. From Grotius's conclusion it follows that the decisions of war must eventuate from a full and wide public debate. Once these basic principles are in place, all that remains is to articulate the criteria that will guide the public debate and limit the acts of war.

Perhaps the finest example of how these two dicta lead to the just war criteria is Jefferson's Declaration of Independence. Faced with the task of justifying a war, Jefferson began with Grotius--"a decent respect to the opinions of mankind requires that they should declare the causes which impel them to the separation." Next he addressed the six relevant *ius ad bellum* criteria (omitting probability of success), and culminates with Cicero--"We must, therefore, acquiesce in the necessity, which denounces our Separation, and hold them, as we hold the rest of mankind, Enemies in War, in Peace Friends."

The second secular route to the just war criteria is via Aristotle's principle of double effect; this is the route pioneered by Aquinas in his *Summa Theologica*. Unfortunately this is a somewhat confused route because Aquinas fails to mention Aristotle's principle in IIa-IIae, q40, "War," the question in which Aquinas addresses war explicitly by adducing three of the six *ius ad bellum* criteria (competent authority, just cause, and right intention). In order to find the principle of double effect, one must look here and there in *Summa Theologica* (for example, Ia-IIae, q1, 13; q6, 4; q12, 4; q18, 6; IIa-IIae, q43, 3; q64, 7-8), everywhere that is except in question 40. In particular, one must wade through twenty-four additional questions before reaching number 64, "On Homicide," articles 7 and 8; and then one must understand the parallel between justified homicide and justified war. If the principle of double effect found in question 64, articles 7 and 8, explains why some homicides are justified and others are not, then precisely the same reasoning explains why some wars are justified and others are not.

Since few possess either sufficient patience or interest, most come away from Aquinas thinking that the just war criteria have no other basis than Augustine's observation that "War and conquest are a sad necessity in the eyes of men of principle, yet it would be still more unfortunate if wrongdoers should dominate just men" (*City of God* 4, ch. 15), and several Biblical citations such as, "He [the magistrate] beareth not the sword in vain for he is God's minister, an avenger to execute wrath upon him that doth evil" (Rom. 13:4). However, once this formidable obstacle is overcome, one discovers that Aristotle's principle provides by far the firmer ground upon which to establish the just war criteria, avoiding as it does not only the problems of an appeal to religion but also all the unresolved complexities of natural law and the language of human rights.

Aristotle's most complete exposition of the principle of double effect is found in his *Physics* (197^{b}20):

> Hence it is clear that events which (1) belong to the general class of things that may come to pass for the sake of something, (2) do not come to pass for the sake of what actually results, and (3) have an external cause, may be described by the phrase "from spontaneity." These "spontaneous" events are said to be "from chance" if they have the further characteristics of being the objects of deliberate intention and due to agents capable of that mode of action.

A simpler, more direct formulation is also found in the *Rhetoric*: "it happens that any given thing usually has both good and bad consequences" (1399^{a}10. See also 1363^{a}24, 1369^{b}21, 1391^{b}7, and *Poetics* 1461^{a}5.).

The most important point to note about the principle of double effect is that it is neither a religious nor a moral principle--it is a physical or empirical one. It is found in Aristotle's *Physics,* not in his *Metaphysics* or *Ethics.* As a physical principle, it merely restates the obvious: when agents act, their actions do not produce a single intended effect; rather they produce a "double" effect. That is, an agent's actions produce both intended and unintended consequences, both desirable and undesirable effects, both good and bad results. Driving an automobile saves time and money and greatly enhances human freedom; it also pollutes the environment.[2] The moral implications of this empirical fact are equally straightforward. In our contingent world all actions must be carefully considered so as to maximize the desirable and minimize the undesirable consequences. Careful consideration, in turn, requires a commitment not only to reason but also to reasoned debate.

A commitment to reason is both obvious and indispensable. The commitment to reasoned debate may be less obvious, given our Kantian belief in the moral autonomy of the individual; nonetheless it is equally indispensable. Since no individual possesses either the knowledge or the objectivity to balance out all the desirable and undesirable consequences of his actions, he must rely upon others to assist him in his investigations. He must seek out those who are affected by his actions and debate the pros and cons, the good and the bad, the intended and the unintended consequences of his actions. Moreover this debate must not only be full and wide ranging; more important, it must be organized. It must be guided by a set of criteria that will ensure that all the relevant questions are asked and, one hopes, answered. When the actions under debate pertain to war, the relevant questions are listed in the just war criteria: Is the cause just? Is there a right intention? Is war the last resort? And so on.

There is of course no need for anyone to debate the justness of their actions. As noted, both individuals and societies can easily abdicate their responsibilities to debate the causes and consequences of a war--either by blindly accepting the pronouncements of religious (or ideological) authorities, by claiming that all wars are immoral a priori, or by sheer indifference. Indeed, the temptation to avoid such a painful debate, to avoid contemplating the horrible images of war, is almost overwhelming; nonetheless the renunciation of the responsibility to arrive at well-considered judgments concerning specific wars through reasoned debate, while understandable, is difficult to accept.

Assuming, therefore, that we do not wish to renounce our responsibilities, then what other recourse do we possess other than to debate the questions raised by the just war criteria? Freeing ourselves from the entanglements of religion and grounding the debate either upon the infirm sands of natural law--that halfway house between religion and science--or preferably upon the empirical reality of Aristotle's principle of double effect, we must debate the justice of our cause and compare it with that of the other side. We must examine our intentions and the competence of our authority. We must calculate the probability of success and the proportionality of our ends. In sum, we must overcome the ridicule and disrepute into which the criteria have fallen, understand their purely secular, indeed empirical foundations, and in all humility struggle with the wrenching debate that they provoke.

III. JUST WAR THINKING AND THE EUROPEAN TRADITION

Having spent the last few pages disentangling the criteria from religion in general, and Christianity in particular, we are now in a position to evaluate the unique achievements of the European just war tradition. Specifically it is possible to acknowledge three achievements that distinguish the European from all other traditions: the secularization of the criteria, the exhaustive systematization of the criteria, and most stunning of all, the realization that just wars are not merely a matter of justice, but of charity as well.

Secularization of the just war criteria is unique to the European tradition. All other traditions continue to base their just war thinking upon religious or ideological grounds. Furthermore, as argued in the previous section, it is not just secularization that distinguishes the European tradition. In reviving Aristotle's principle of double effect, Aquinas put the just war criteria upon firm empirical foundations, thereby decisively severing the link between religion and the criteria. After Aquinas it was possible to debate the justice of a war without ever mentioning a god, the divine will, or citing a passage from a sacred scripture--indeed without even mentioning that thinly disguised deity, natural law.

The exhaustive systematization of the criteria is the fruit of four hundred years of effort by canon lawyers. During the late Middle Ages, when the Church's prestige was at its height, the feudal barons were constantly demanding that the Church sanction their interminable wars. In response to these incessant and inopportune demands, between the twelfth and the sixteenth centuries canon lawyers slowly developed the vague dicta of Augustine and the classical authors into the system of precise criteria that now constitutes the just war criteria. As an intellectual and political achievement, this systematization is a unique accomplishment. Moreover our current system of international law is also dependent in large measure upon the success that the canon lawyers had in systematizing the just war criteria. Since war is the single most important topic in international law, norms of international conduct could not be developed unless the criteria for evaluating the justice and injustice of specific wars were articulated, which is precisely what the canon lawyers did.

And finally the European tradition has broadened the foundations of the just war criteria by introducing a concern for charity. From Augustine on, questions of war and peace have been seen to involve more than the matter of justice. To seek peace and justice is never sufficient. Simple vengeance, after all, may also be an act of justice and result in peace. Acts of war, however, must also be acts of love. Consequently it is no accident that Aquinas discusses war in the section immediately after his discussion of "Charity," in a section which the Blackfriars have entitled the "Consequences of Charity."

An unjust war is of course always a violation of charity. What is less easily seen, however, is that even a just war loses its luster when it is not animated by charity. When love for the enemy (Matt 5:44, Luke 6:27, 35) is the motivating force, and the desire to transform enmity into amity by returning the discordant factions of the community to greater harmony is the principal purpose of the war, then the war has moved beyond simple justice and into the realm of charity. And once one has moved into the realm of charity, both the sterile controversies over traditional rights and duties that marked so many wars from ancient times down to the French revolution and the equally sterile appeals to *raisons d'état* in more modern times are revealed for what they really are--naked pride clothing itself in convenient pretense. Moving beyond justice to charity, needless to say, represents a significant and unique contribution to just war thinking.

In conclusion, despite the fact that the just war criteria have been ridiculed, misunderstood, and ignored for four hundred years or more, there is really no alternative. Locked into absolute certainty, both the crusader and the pacifist have nothing either interesting or relevant to say about the justice of specific wars. To adopt either attitude is to remove oneself from the debate. Debate, however, is precisely what the just war criteria are all about--a disciplined, structured, reasoned debate that leads to well-considered judgments. In the end there are but two options. One may opt for either the silent certainty of the holy war and pacifist mentalities or the anguished debate of the just war criteria.

NOTES

1. An interesting example of a secular development of the just war criteria is to be found in a remarkable set of speeches given by then Secretary of State George Shultz and Secretary of Defense Caspar Weinberger in 1984. In these speeches the two men developed a version of the just war criteria as guidelines for the deployment of American military forces, a question of burning interest after the truck bombing of the Marine billet in Beirut.

2. A modern articulation of Aristotle's principle is found in Hannah Arendt's essay "On Violence."

> "Violence, being instrumental by nature, is rational to the extent that it is effective in reaching the end that must justify it. And since when we act we never know with any certainty the eventual consequences of what we are doing, violence can remain rational only if it pursues short-term goals" (Arendt 1972, 176).

She also gives a more elaborate example:

> "The federal government promotes school integration in the South by cutting off federal funds in cases of flagrant noncompliance. In one such instance, $200,000 of annual aid was withheld. 'Of the total, $175,000 went directly to Negro schools. . . . Whites promptly raised taxes to replace the other $25,000.' In short, what is supposed to help Negro education actually has a 'crushing impact' on their existing school system and no impact at all on white schools" (Arendt 1972, 197; the quotes in the example are from a story by Neil Maxwell in the *Wall Street Journal* of 8 August 1968).

REFERENCES

Aquinas, Thomas. 1964. *Summa Theologica*. Blackfriars edition. New York: McGraw-Hill.

Arendt, Hannah. 1972. "On Violence." In *Crises of the Republic*. New York: Harcourt, Brace, Jovanovich.

Cicero. 1967. *Cicero on Moral Obligation: A New Translation of Cicero's 'De Officiis'*. Trans. John Higginbotham. Los Angles and Berkeley: University of California Press.

"Convention Relating to the Opening of Hostilities." 1909. In the *Consolidated Treaty Series* vol. 205. Ed. Clive Parry. Dobbs Ferry, NY: Oceana.

Erasmus. 1957. *Ten Colloquies*. Trans. Craig R. Thompson. New York: Liberal Arts Press.

Grotius, Hugo. 1925. *De Jure Belli ac Pacis Libri Tres II*. Trans. Francis W. Kelsey. Oxford: Clarendon.

Homer. 1982. *Homer's Iliad*. Trans. Denison Bingham Hull. Scottsdale, Arizona.

National Conference of Catholic Bishops. May 3, 1983. "The Challenge of Peace: God's Promise and Our Response." Washington, D.C. For additional reading on the just war criteria, the bishops provide a good selection on p. 27, note 31. An alternate source is the United States Catholic Conference, May 19, 1983, "The Challenge of Peace," *Origins* 13 (1).

Potter, Ralph B., Jr. 1970. "The Moral Logic of War."
    McCormick Quarterly 23:203-33. Reprinted in *Peace and
    War*. Ed. Charles R. Beitz and Theodore Herman. 1973.
    San Francisco: W. H. Freeman.
Shultz, George. 1984. "The Ethics of Power: Address at the
    Convocation of Yeshiva University in New York on
    December 9, 1984." Department of State Bulletin 85 (2095).
    Washington, DC: United States Government Printing Office.
Sun Tzu. 1963. *The Art of War*. Trans. Samuel B. Griffith, with
    foreword by B. H. Liddell Hart. Oxford: Clarendon.
Weinberger, Caspar. 1984. "Speech before the National Press Club
    on 28 November 1984." *New York Times* 29 November
    1984, p. A5.

Can Modern Wars Be Just?

DONALD A. WELLS

Preface

The moral problem of war is that it obligates us to do abroad what we have established is criminal to do at home: to kill neighbors whom we have never met, to destroy their homes, desecrate their national treasures, plunder their natural resources, and hold their innocent men, women, and children hostage. War entails that we engage in acts that expose the innocent to hunger, disease, wounds, and death.

We live in a world where war is not illegal and where the practice of war is seen as an extension of politics. It has rarely been believed that wars would ever be made unlawful. But historically it has been hoped that rules could be established concerning the reasons for going to war and setting limits to the means used to wage war. "Just war" theory, as established by Augustine in the fourth century, was an effort to provide moral criteria by which war makers could justify their acts. Resolutions of The Hague congresses in 1899 and 1907 and Geneva International Red Cross conferences from 1864 to the present have proposed limits to what should be sanctioned in war. The Nuremberg and Tokyo war crimes tribunals presumed that these Hague and Geneva resolutions had the force of law. In the absence of any judicial body to identify offenses or to impose sanctions, nations commonly feel neither legally nor morally bound to comply in moments of military emergency.

The vitality of "just war" theory after fifteen hundred years is testimony to a human concern to justify both the reasons for going to war and the means by which modern wars are fought. This brief essay is an attempt to explore whether the appeal to these basically moral criteria can enable us to claim that our wars are morally just.

We live in a world where no international law exists that makes going to war a crime. When nations go to war there are no international laws obligating them to be humane, to spare the helpless and unarmed, to refrain from destroying national treasures, or to show any sense of moderation. To be sure both The Hague and Geneva conferences urged through resolutions that moderation be shown. These resolutions, however, lacked the status of law. Nonetheless it was assumed since ancient times that limits existed to what should be permitted in war and the expression "laws of war" goes back at least to Thucydides, Aristotle, and Cicero. The Athenians criticized the Spartans for being bloodthirsty in war. Aristotle affirmed that war against barbarians was always just (*Politics* 1, ch. 8:1256). Cicero urged that laws of war be obeyed so that men might be better than brutes in their fighting. He reminded his contemporaries that since war was a human enterprise it ought, therefore, to be subject to humanizing laws. He concluded that while wars to protect property were just, wars for the expansion of property were not (*Offices* 1, sect. 12). Furthermore, he observed that it is "a great man's duty . . . to single out the guilty for punishment, to spare the many" (*Offices* 1, sect. 24). It was less than clear who was to listen to these suggestions and who was to implement them. They were basically moral urgings.

Most historians have portrayed war as one of the legitimate ways by which states are administered, offenders punished, and national aims achieved. As a consequence early criticisms of war were not against its use in principle, but rather against either the ends for which the war was fought or the means by which these ends were pursued. The criticism of ends implied that some wars ought not to be fought at all. Few illustrations from the past exist, however, to support the conclusion that national leaders refrained from war because they realized that their ends were unworthy. Criticism of means implied that even in a proper war warriors had to obey certain laws. The belief that there were laws of war entailed that there could be crimes of war. The crimes could consist either of waging a war for shallow reasons or waging a proper war by improper means. But no adjudicating body existed to enforce these limits.

St. Ambrose and his distinguished pupil St. Augustine invented "just war" theory to explain to Christians who had previously rejected war altogether, that there were now conditions under which war would get a divine blessing. With the conversion of Constantine, Christians who previously had only a heavenly kingdom, now had an earthly kingdom to protect. The matter of war was considered by Augustine under two questions: 1) Under what conditions was it just to declare a war? (*ius ad bellum*), and 2)

By what means was it just to wage a war? (*ius in bello*). In effect Christian just war theory was a moral effort based on theological premises. For almost a thousand years the Roman Catholic Church was the court that made these judgments. To the present day just war theory has moral and theological roots. In a Holy Roman Empire it could be maintained that these basically religious criteria were at the same time legal rules governing both the reasons for going to war and the means by which a war should be fought.

The present world, however, is not a unified place and even the United Nations and its International Court of Justice are unable to rule on so-called violations of war. The UN can urge that wars be entered only as a last resort and then only under UN jurisdiction, but it has no authority, save what the member nations give, to urge negotiations and to deplore by sanctions and resolutions certain acts of war. The moral problem of war is that it permits and rewards acts which domestically we consider criminal: killing our neighbors, stealing their property, invading their hegemony, desecrating their treasures, and wounding innocent men, women, and children. Since the Roman Empire became officially Christian, and it was not expected that Constantine would give up the historic right to go to war, just war theory was an effort to set moral limits to acts which previously had no legal limits, but which in traditional Christian doctrine were morally forbidden.

1. What Are Just Reasons for Declaring War?

Just war theory accepts war as a moral possibility. With regard to the question of the declaration of war several conditions have been proposed. The end needs to be sufficiently worthy to justify the human slaughter and property damage wars entail. The declaration must be made as a last resort after all possible negotiations have been carried out. And this declaration must be made by the "duly constituted authority." In Question 10 of *Questions Concerning the Heptateuch,* Augustine proposed several ends that he considered justification for war: preservation of the well-being of the state, punishment of neighbor nations that refuse to make amends for wrongs committed by their subjects, and retaking what another had wrongfully taken. While he deplored the restless ambition that promoted wars for sovereignty (*City of God* 3, sect. 4), he believed that there were conditions under which it was just to extend empire. If this were not permitted, then nations already under the power of a wicked ruler could not righteously be aided in revolt. Thus a war to take land away from a tyrant was just (*City of God* 4, para. 15). Augustine had confidence that the ruler of the Holy Roman Empire would know who the tyrants were. In the present world of sovereign nations each nation presumes that its enemy is the tyrant. In any event soldiers act at the request of their civil authority, and when they do so they are not culpable for their war acts. Even a soldier commanded to war by an unrighteous king is innocent, "because his position makes obedience a duty" (*Reply to Faustus the Manichaean* 22, para 75).

International jurists during the sixteenth through the eighteenth centuries paid special attention to the question of what ends were worthy enough to justify war. The religious roots of just war theory were evident in the writings of two of the earliest jurists, both of whom were professors of theology: Franciscus da Victoria (1486-1546) and Francisco Suarez (1548-1617). They made suggestions as to worthy ends that they believed, initially, to be based on actual practice. Balthasar Ayala (1548-1612) included in his list of just ends the defense of empire, coming to the aid of friends and allies, getting back what has been taken from you, putting down a revolt, and taking vengeance for a wrong unjustly inflicted (*On the Law of War* 1, ch. 2). Francisco Suarez said that defensive war is always just, yet even offensive war may be militarily required (*Three Theological Virtues: On Charity* disp. 13, sect. 1). The list supplied by Alberico Gentili (1552-1608) was similar, and he affirmed that just wars can be either defensive or offensive. He stated further that in most cases justice will be on both sides in wars for national gain (*On the Law of War* 1, ch. 6, para. 48). Hugo Grotius (1583-1645) considered defense of self and property to be just causes, although there may be occasions when it would be praiseworthy not to take advantage of the right to war. In general, he proposed that,

> "It is not, then, contrary to the nature of society to look out for oneself and advance one's own interests, provided the rights of others are not infringed; and consequently the use of force which does not violate the rights of others is not unjust" (*On the Law of War and Peace* 1, ch. 1).

By the end of the eighteenth century discussion of the justice of ends, in the medieval sense, had ceased to be relevant. William Paley (1743-1805) stated the matter as one of national interest and not of moral virtue. He considered the just and unjust causes as follows:

> "The justifying causes of war are, deliberate invasions of right, and the necessity of maintaining such a balance of power amongst neighboring nations, as that no single state, or confederacy of states, be strong enough to overwhelm the rest. The objects of just war are, precaution, defense, or reparation. . . . The unjustifiable motives of war, are the family alliances, the personal friendships, or the personal quarrels of princes . . . the extension of territory, or of trade, or accidental weakness of a neighboring or rival nation" (*Moral and Political Philosophy* 4).

The relatively simple current conventional thinking on war states that any defensive war is just and any offensive war is unjust. The judgment as to whether a war is defensive or offensive is made by each nation to suit its interests. The United Nations may condemn an act of invasion, but sovereign nations reserve the right to make the final decision as to who is defending and who is invading. The problem has always been to find an authoritative body that can determine who started a particular war.[1] With the advent of the strategy of "preemptive war," the conventional criterion of who fired the first shot was no longer sufficient. The distinguished British authority on international law, L. Oppenheim, remarked that confusion had been generated by the Nuremberg Tribunal appeal to the Paris Pact as having outlawed war. If war had been outlawed, he noted, there would be no reason to have laws for its proper use. If war was forbidden, it would be inconsistent to claim that rules governed its legitimate practice. He noted further that a general sentiment existed in favor of denying to "aggressors" any protection at all from laws of war. Yet he cautioned,

> "At the same time in view of the humanitarian character of a substantial part of the rule of war it is imperative that during war these rules should be mutually observed regardless of the legality of the war" (Oppenheim 1952, vol. 2:217-218).

International jurists attempted to discover whether there were clearly unjust reasons for going to war. In sections 11 and 12 of *On the Indians,* Franciscus da Victoria affirmed that wars for religion were not just. Ayala agreed with Victoria and stated that not even the pope nor the Roman emperor could justify a war against infidels merely because they were not Christian (*On the Law of War* 1, ch. 2 para. 28-29). Gentili agreed but doubted that the proscription had much support in fact (*On the Law of War* 1, ch. 10. para. 71). Francisco Suarez supported this judgment on religious wars (*Three Theological Virtues: On Charity* disp. 13, sect. 1, para. 7). It was unfortunate that at the same time the clerics at Toledo had already decreed that heretics should be punished by war. During the lifetime of Aquinas three of the nine Crusades were carried out with the support of Pope Innocent IV and the Council of Lyon. As a consequence Thomas did not indict religious wars. Indeed a century later Giovani da Legnano (d. 1383), professor of canon law at the University of Bologna, still justified wars against infidels (*Law of War* ch. 12). Are wars for political ideology in the same category? It is germane to remember that the Nuremberg Tribunal considered that the attempt to exterminate a people on grounds of religious, ethnic, racial, or political identity was a "crime against humanity." A United Nations resolution of 1948 named such acts "genocide."

Grotius listed as unacceptable some of the reasons currently in vogue: fear of a neighbor; the desire for richer land owned by another; the desire to rule over others for their own good, though against their wills; and the claim to be the self-appointed leader of the world (*On the Law of War and Peace* 2, ch. 13, sect. 5, 7, 11-13). Samuel Rachel (1628-1691) concluded that most wars of the past had been unjust and "not far removed from robbery" (*Law of Nature* sect. 39). By the time of Emmerich Vattel (1714-1767) it was normal to conclude that nations did not even have to declare a war, let alone think up any supposed just reason for waging it (*The Law* ch. 3, para. 27).

Beginning with Augustine, and with little objection down to the seventeenth century, the rule was that only "duly constituted authorities" should make the declaration. Until the rise of democratic aspirations this authority was assumed to be the king or prince. The medieval and modern jurists all agreed: Victoria, Ayala, Suarez, Pierino Belli (1502-1579), Johann Textor (1638-1701), Samuel Pufendorf (1632-1694), Vattel, and Cornelius Bynkerschoek (1673-1743). It was generally denied that any world organization could or should take away the national right to declare war. The importance of the declaration of war rested on the presumption that if there were any laws of war, they would then officially take effect. This announcement had the further advantage of providing a delay between the declaration and the beginning of the war, during which good sense might prevent the war from occurring at all. By 1836, however, the international jurist, Henry Wheaton, noted that the practice of declaring war had virtually ceased. Not only was surprise a military advantage, but the only serious reason for making the declaration of war was to make claims for reparation in a peace treaty (*Elements of International Law* IV, para 297). Between 1770 and 1870 there were over eighty occasions in Europe alone where wars were fought without a declaration ever being made (Davis 1980). Indeed most of the three hundred wars fought since the end of World War II, including the thirty in which the United States has been involved, were never declared.

In spite of this general dismissal of the declaration of war, interest has remained in whether the medieval requirement has been satisfied that wars be fought only as a last resort. Chapter I, article 2, paragraph 3 of the United Nations Charter urges all members to "settle their international disputes by peaceful means." Paragraph 4 states that "all Members shall refrain in their international relations from the threat or use of force against the territorial integrity or political independence of any state." Chapter V, article 24 gives to the Security Council primary responsibility for the maintenance of international peace. Chapter VII, article 33 urges that parties to a potential dispute

> "shall, first of all, seek a solution by negotiation, enquiry, mediation, conciliation, arbitration, judicial settlement, resort to regional agencies or arrangements, or other peaceful means of their own choice."

Debate was vigorous in the U.S. Congress over whether negotiations had been sufficiently pursued in the Persian Gulf. Forty-seven U.S. senators believed that negotiations had not been given sufficient time. Indeed there was concern that the secretary-general of the United Nations was not doing the negotiations and doubt that the ultimatums U.S. Secretary of State James Baker delivered to Iraqi Foreign Minister Tariq Aziz were negotiations in any reasonable sense. Many congresspersons were suggesting that it was not too late to go back to negotiation. Of special relevance in the Gulf crisis is the question whether the unconditional rejection of linkage by the Bush administration constitutes a rejection of negotiation.

A more radical interpretation of the "last resort" premise was taken at the Nuremberg Trials in the charge of "crimes against the peace" against both Germany and Japan for going to war at all at that time. The Axis offense, according to the Nuremberg judges, was not that they went to war prematurely, but that they went to war at all. The just war dictum that wars not be entered into except as a last resort is important because it presupposes that we have good reason for going to war at all. What is unclear is whether the parties to the dispute should be permitted to determine when negotiations will no longer be fruitful.

2. The Means of War.

Two criteria were developed by which warriors were to judge whether their means were just. (1) A principle of proportionality stated that the havoc caused by war should not exceed the supposed gain to be achieved. This dictum was commonly linked with the prevalent doctrine of "military necessity:" no more damage should be inflicted than would be militarily necessary to win. For example it was affirmed that soldiers hors de combat, being no military threat, ought not to be killed or further wounded. Obviously in the absence of any measuring scale, individual military or political leaders could differ widely as to when too much damage had been done. Effort was made in the medieval period to ban certain weapons or strategies of war as being excessive. Among the excessive weapons were poison, incendiaries, and the crossbow. Among excessive strategies were declaring a war of "no quarter" or assaulting civilian centers. (2) A combatant-noncombatant distinction was affirmed. War should be waged only against armed soldiers. Soldiers hors de combat and unarmed citizens were innocent and ought not to be slain.

A. CAN PROPORTIONALITY BE MEASURED?

Franciscus da Victoria had raised this matter at the time of the Spanish war against the American Indians. He had asked, "What kind of stress is lawful in a just war?" While he maintained that the prince could do whatever was required to defend the commonwealth, there were limits.

"If some one city cannot be recaptured without greater evils befalling the State, such as devastation of many cities, great slaughter of human beings . . . it is indubitable that the Prince is bound rather to give up his own rights and abstain from war" (*On the Indians* sect. 3, para. 15-18).

What was lacking was some wise Solomon to make this calculation. Suarez was convinced that it would be unreasonable to inflict grave harm when the injustice was slight (*Three Theological Virtues: On Charity* disp. 13, sect. 4). Nations had a right of reprisal, but they needed to know when such reprisal would be excessive. Textor denied that military necessity could be used to justify "abhorrent acts. . . . Some arithmetical proportion should exist between the hurt . . . and the warlike licence allowed" (*Synopsis of the Law of Nations* ch. 17, sect. 3). Cornelius Bynkerschoek concluded, "In my opinion every force is lawful in war. . . . Does it matter what means we use?" (*Questions of Public Law* ch. 1, para. 3). Medieval church councils endeavored to resolve such questions by naming "excessive" weapons or strategies. Weapons such as poison and incendiaries were listed as prohibited. The strategy of waging a war of "no quarter" was also banned. Richard Zouche (1590-1661) condemned the act of the Spanish in poisoning the French water supply (*An Exposition of Fecial Law and Procedure* sect. 10, para. 5). He also condemned the action of the Italians who sent infected prostitutes into French military camps. Vattel attempted to classify treacheries by degrees. Poison was more revolting than assassination, but poisoned weapons were less objectionable than poisoning the water supply (*The Law* ch. 8, para. 155-56).

International congresses in the nineteenth and twentieth centuries made further efforts to provide examples of excessive or disproportionate weapons or strategies. The Declaration of St. Petersburg in 1868 recommended a ban on explosive bullets weighing less than four hundred grams. A Declaration of Brussels in 1874 urged a ban on the use of poison, poisoned bullets, and chemical and biological weapons. The congresses at The Hague in 1899 and 1907 proposed bans on expanding bullets, asphyxiating or deleterious gases, biologicals, the dropping of explosives from balloons, and the firing of torpedoes that remain lethal after they miss their mark. Conventions of the International Red Cross in 1864 and 1868 had urged humane care of prisoners of war. A Geneva Protocol of 1925 advocated a ban on noxious chemicals and biological weapons. On several occasions the General Assembly of the United Nations made similar efforts to illustrate what disproportional weapons might be. A resolution of 1972 banned napalm and other incendiaries; a resolution of 1981 banned "particularly inhumane weapons" including fragmentation bombs, incendiaries, and booby traps; and a resolution of 1982 proposed a ban on the manufacture and stockpiling of chemical and biological weapons. In 1982 several resolutions proposed a ban on the manufacture, stockpiling, and threats to use nuclear weapons. Both The Hague and Geneva congresses had proposed that unfortified cities be protected from bombing.

Utilizing these Hague and Geneva resolutions the Nuremberg Tribunal accused Germans and Japanese of violating laws of war and of conducting war with excessive slaughter. Such offenses were called "war crimes" and "crimes against humanity," and the commission of them meant that on the German and Japanese side the war had not been waged in accordance with "laws of war." The primary offense named at those trials was the systematic extermination of persons in prisoner of war camps. The judges believed that laws existed to protect soldiers hors de combat, and that the deliberate extermination of civilians violated the just war criterion to the effect that the innocent must never be deliberately slain. The problem of measuring when excessive means had been used proved as difficult for the Nuremberg judges as it had been for the medieval jurists. In the trial of Wilhelm List and others under Control Council Law No. 10 the tribunal ruled that the Germans acted excessively in killing fifty to one hundred Communists for every German soldier slain. Yet the Tribunal left unanswered what a proportional number might have been. General Lanz on trial in Greece was found guilty of excess for having issued a reprisal order to shoot ten Greeks for every act of sabotage to the underwater cable. Was there a proportional number?

The medieval ban on certain weapons of their day seems unrealistic today considering the kinds of weapons now in military arsenals: chemical and biological bombs, napalm, fragmentation bombs, and nuclear bombs, quite apart from conventional carpet bombing strategies with nonnuclear explosives. Can the two just war criteria of sparing the innocent and avoiding what The Hague congresses called "superfluous injury," or "unnecessary suffering" be satisfied by warriors today? Can warriors today defend the use of modern weapons of war by appeal to the just war criterion of proportionality?

B. DO INNOCENTS EXIST IN WAR?

The medieval church councils believed that they were implementing just war criteria when they insisted that there were people who ought not to be slain in war. The combatant-noncombatant distinction needed to be maintained in a war justly fought. Historically these innocents included old men, women, children, clergy, farmers, and merchants. Victoria claimed that even in wars against the Turks it was not allowed to kill women and children (*On the Indians* para. 37). At the same time he urged that it was not permitted to kill foreigners, clerics, guests, or members of religious orders. Belli noted that this principle was little observed (*Treatise on Military Matters and Warfare* ch. 9, sect. 1-7). While Grotius approved of the protection of women and children, he noted that common practice was to kill them along with soldiers and that the laws of war even sanctioned this (*On the Law of War and Peace* 3, ch. 4, sect. 9). While Vattel thought that even though in war every citizen of the enemy country was an enemy, women and children still ought not to be killed (*Law of Nations* ch. 8, para. 145). In ancient times wars of "no quarter" were common and the policy of annihilating the total population was accepted war strategy. If practice was any guide, then any claim that there existed a law against slaying any particular group of persons was without foundation.

In the medieval period, through the use of certain flags or pennons and the issuance of certain threats or requests for surrender, rules were created to control both the occasion and the number of persons who could be slain. In wars of "no quarter" the total population could be slaughtered. The refusal of a town to surrender exposed it to the right of the enemy to kill every resident. Victoria raised the question, "Whether in a just war it is lawful to kill, at any rate, all of the guilty?" (*On the Indians* sect. 44-48). His reply was that in war, in the heat of battle, anyone who resists may be slain. But may we continue to kill soldiers after they have surrendered? Victoria thought that in wars against unbelievers it might be expedient to kill everyone. In the case of wars against Christians, however,

> "I think that they may not be killed, not only not all of them, but not even one of them, if the presumption is that they entered the strife in good faith."

But once wars are fought for political, social, economic, or religious ideologies, the temptation exists to treat all opponents as lacking in good faith. Thus negotiations never get started because national leaders are prompted to doubt all enemy offers to negotiate. Grotius extended the right to kill after surrender to cover not simply soldiers who had born arms, but everyone who resided in the enemy territory. Even prisoners of war could be killed (*On the Law of War and Peace* 3, sect. 12, 14). Textor denied that soldiers who had surrendered could ever be slain (*Synopsis of the Law of Nations* ch. 18, para. 17, 19). Thus common practice did not seem to support any claim that there was a rule.

Efforts to implement the protection of innocents resulted in declarations at The Hague and Geneva conferences that forbade the bombing of "unfortified" cities. In the event that a military target was adjacent to a civilian center, military leaders were urged to warn the civilians in advance so they could move to safer areas. However, surprise in attack was commonly good military strategy, so that succeeding U.S. Army manuals, including the current 1976 revision of the *Law of Land Warfare*, provided a special "American Rule" whereby the warning could be withheld. Notification is required only "when the situation permits" (*Law of Land Warfare* para. 43). Aerial warfare has posed special problems with efforts to spare noncombatants. Indeed the bombing of civilian centers was such common practice by both the Allies and the Axis in World War II that the Nuremberg Tribunal did not consider it to be a violation of the rules of war. One consequence of air force strategy was that almost 50 percent of the casualties in World War II were civilian. In Korea civilian casualties were about 84 percent and in Vietnam about 90 percent.[2] Given such civilian casualties, could the just war criterion of sparing the innocent be met?

In the medieval period soldiers occasionally killed a noncombatant by accident. Jesuit clerics proposed a "principle of the double effect" whereby warriors were excused for unintended deaths. Church councils provided penance for soldiers who unintentionally killed the innocent, so that guilt could be absolved. Obviously as weapons became more powerful and less discriminating the number of such unintended deaths increased. Moral theory ever since Aristotle provided excuses for unintended or chance results. We were responsible only for what we had intended and for what we could have foreseen. War posed special problems, since almost any military strategy entailed the death of both soldiers and the innocent. Many of the consequences of war strategy were unforeseeable, but once we knew the effects of new weapons, did it follow that we knew in advance that bad effects would result? Could we still appeal to just war theory to justify our acts? The Jesuit doctrine of the "double effect" provided that moral acts with both good and bad effects could be forgiven provided the agent did not intend the bad effect. It was assumed that the good effect followed from the good act and was not a consequence of the bad effect. On this theory Thomas Aquinas had difficulty supporting self-defense, since the good effect of saving your own life followed from the bad effect of taking the life of another, rather than from any initial moral act. Once again just war theorists faced the problem of calculation required by just war theory; we need some yardstick to determine that the harm we cause is unintended, unavoidable, and, hence, excusable.

The current military language to describe this situation is "collateral damage." Such damage is purportedly unintended, unavoidable, accidental, and deplorable. Modern military strategists talk about civilian deaths and the destruction of nonmilitary targets as collateral. The presumption of such language is that the damage is not intended and that it is not excessive. Aerial bombing in World War II consisted of "carpet bombing" civilian centers, with the result that half the damage was to persons and places which just war theory declares protected. In the Persian Gulf war, military leaders spent time explaining how precise their weapons are, so that the listener got the impression that bombs are so "smart" that only in the rarest of cases do the innocent suffer. Unfortunately in wartime the news blackout is so effective that we do not know until all the damage has been done whether what is called "collateral damage" is indeed minor, let alone unintended. Just war criteria require, however, that we know beforehand that the acts of war we contemplate performing will not be disproportional. Quite apart from so-called smart bombs, it is still the case that most of the rest of the weapons in current arsenals are of the "dumb" variety. Indeed the results of conventional "carpet bombing" with "dumb" bombs, and of fragmentation and incendiary explosives, are so vast and indiscriminate that it is not evident that the warrior can dismiss civilian deaths as merely collateral. George Kent has documented the vast number of children casualties, both intended and unintended, which follow from wars (Kent 1990). Can we calculate these deaths as proportional? Can such deaths be explained as unintended and collateral? Can it still be argued that we wage "just" wars?

Conclusions

Can we meet the requirements of just war theory at the present time so that we can properly prove that we are waging just wars? Can we demonstrate that we have a just reason for going to war at all? Can we show that we did so only as a last resort? Can we make the necessary calculations to prove that the consequences of our acts of war are not excessive? Can we prove that we did not kill innocents intentionally? Can we show that of all the alternatives we faced, war was the most humane and moral option? These are questions we must answer if we are to defend the claim that we have been waging a just war. To what neutral adjudicating body do we make these claims? Whom do we have to persuade before we can rest assured that what we do in war is just?

The claim that a war is just for our side and unjust for our opponent was a problem faced by the Nuremberg Tribunal after World War II. If there are laws of war, then the breaking of those laws will be crimes of war no matter what nationality of soldiers are involved. The Nuremberg judges derived the offenses called "war crimes" from declarations made at the two Hague congresses. They derived the offenses called "crimes against humanity" from declarations made at the various Geneva International Red Cross conferences. They derived the offenses called "crimes against the peace" from the Paris Peace Pact of 1928. In a very real sense the judgments at Nuremberg and Tokyo were judgments that the Axis declared war for unjust reasons, went to war prematurely, and once in the war fought it at some points by unjust means. But did the judgments imply that the Allies declared the war justly and waged it by just means? In *The Case Against Nazi War Criminals,* Judge Robert Jackson expressed the hope that the tribunal would not judge Germans and Japanese for any crimes for which the tribunal would not be willing to judge the Allies. We know that the tribunal did not prosecute any of the Allied soldiers or leaders. There is a wealth of writing by legal, military, religious, and moral scholars that raise serious doubts that the trials rested on firm foundations.[3]

The calculations that must be made concerning just war require the kind of neutral judge we are familiar with in domestic courts of law. The Nuremberg judges believed that they could make these calculations. Current debate in the United Nations is endeavoring to assess whether in the war in the Persian Gulf either the US or Iraq is exceeding both proportionality and the mandate against deliberate civilian deaths. What measuring device is available? Have too many civilians been killed? Are their deaths excusable on grounds of the double effect or what we call "collateral damage?" We know that some calculation is required under just war theory. Can we now determine whether the soldiers on any side of a given war are or are not waging a just war by just means? Military leaders who are expected to win a war for their side are in no position to make the required calculations to show that they have not used excessive means or that the damage to civilians is really collateral. National leaders are not neutral judges. Indeed it was understood by international jurists at the end of the eighteenth century that the requirements of sovereign nationalism were inconsistent with the hope for laws of war, and, hence, with our capacity as nationalists to make just war claims.

It is too easy to forget that the laws of war and the criteria of just war theory were written for a time when the weapons of war were relatively simple, and when it was believed that we possessed a wise and neutral judge. Even in World War I the Russian cavalry went faster and farther than the best Russian tanks. Cannon projectiles might contain as much as fifty pounds of explosive. Our airplanes now move with unthought of speed and our intercontinental missiles allow no time for just war theorists to calculate. Incendiaries, gas, chemicals, and explosives, which historically had been banned by just war theorists, are all standard weapons in arsenals. Although military manuals still speak of chivalry as if it could be an ameliorating factor--including the U.S. *Law of Land Warfare* (para. 3a, FM 27-10)--this language of knighthood can no longer be applied. Indeed if medieval knights had done battle with flame throwers, fragmentation bombs, and airplanes the term chivalry would never have been created. What we do on battlefields today is not war as imagined by just war theorists. This is especially poignant as we attempt to show that the havoc we cause is not disproportional and that civilian casualties are merely collateral. There is an important difference between the assertion that there are laws of war, the breaking of which would be legal crimes, and the historical claim of just war theorists that these are moral offenses.

We know what should be done and what should not be done. Noncombatants should be spared, unfortified cities should not be bombed, unnecessary suffering should be avoided, the wounded and imprisoned should be cared for, and every alternative short of war should be exhausted first. Can we appeal to the criteria of just war theory today and show that we are waging a war justly? We shall have to set aside, at the outset, the basic requirement that there be an adjudicating body who will hear our case. No such body exists, although the United Nations is surely a good place for nations to make their case. We will need to show that we have a cause so just that it sanctions all the killing which will follow, all the destruction of national treasures, and the devastation of natural resources. And we will need to prove that this worthy end cannot be reached by any means less than war. National leaders seem to have little difficulty persuading themselves that their intentions are worthy, and if history shows anything it is that national leaders have a tendency to jump into war with unseemly haste. Would such a case receive approval from the General Assembly of the United Nations? We might make a case that our means are proportional and that we spare the innocent provided that we eliminate most of the weapons in our arsenals, beginning with our bombing from the air and continuing on to most long-range guns, fragmentation bombs, incendiaries, and chemicals, not to forget nuclear weapons. All of these have been banned by Hague, Geneva, or United Nations resolutions. If any rules exist that identify excess, they come from these bodies. Collateral damage or the excuse of the double effect are not Hague, Geneva, or UN concepts. They are military excuses for the unavoidable catastrophes of war. As long as sovereign nations retain the inalienable right to defend their aims and to be the sole judges of both the ends and means, no manual can ever be written that could guide soldiers to avoid the very excesses The Hague and Geneva declarations prohibit, let alone the far more stringent prerequisites which have to be met before we can utilize the moral language of just war theory.

Postscript on the Gulf War

Much effort was expended by the White House, the State Department, and the Pentagon to keep the American public uninformed about the gulf war. In spite of an almost complete news blackout concerning what was taking place in our name and the number and nature of the casualties of the war, we have enough information from the alternative press and from European news media to make some specific comments on how this war scored on the scale of the just war criteria. Let us concentrate on three matters: 1) Was there a proper declaration and was it conducted as a last resort? 2) Was the havoc caused proportional to the value of the ends to be achieved? and 3) Were the innocent spared? Was the combatant-noncombatant distinction upheld? Was the "collateral damage" minimal, unintended, and unavoidable?

1. WAS THE WAR JUSTLY DECLARED?

President Bush assured us that the war was called for by the United Nations, and although our own Congress never declared war, we were told that a sanction for the war was well established. A reading of the United Nations Security Council resolutions 660 through 678, however, shows that no sanction for the war that followed the January 15, 1991, deadline can be deduced from any of these Security Council actions. On August 2, 1990, Iraq invaded Kuwait and the same day the Security Council condemned the action and called for the immediate and unconditional withdrawal of Iraq to the August 1 position, and for Iraq and Kuwait to begin immediately "intensive negotiations for the resolution of their differences and supports all efforts in this regard, and especially those of the League of Arab States" (Resolution 660). The vote was 14 yeas, 0 nays, and 1 abstention, Yemen. On August 7 our president sent 150,000 US troops to Saudi Arabia. This was in violation of both the United Nations Charter, which calls for peaceful resolutions, and the clear wish of the Security Council to have negotiations pursued. No statement was made or implied in Resolution 660 recommending any military solution. On August 13 the secretary-general of the UN disassociated himself from any use of force. The sending of US troops after five days of no negotiation at all was clearly a violation of the "last resort" clause.

By early January Iraq had repeated several times its offer to withdraw. Third party proposals for withdrawal had been made by the French, the Arab League, and the Soviet Union. For the most part all of these had Iraqi support. President Bush dismissed all these efforts, thus demonstrating his intention not to allow negotiations to be pursued. Furthermore Resolution 678 of November 29, 1990, was not, as President Bush claimed, a UN sanction for the use of military force after the January 15, 1991, deadline. While the initial United States version referred to "all necessary force," the final version read "all necessary means." China threatened to veto the resolution if the word "force" was used. With the term "means" replacing "force," China abstained. Since the concurrence of the five permanent members was required for a valid vote, then it seems to follow that the vote was not a valid one.

Since an abstention is not a vote, let alone a vote in favor, shouldn't Resolution 678 have been declared void? Professor Richard Falk is one of the few legal scholars to have raised this question. In any event Resolution 678 was not a sanction for war after January 15, 1991.

2. WAS THE WAR FOUGHT PROPORTIONALLY?

The television media emphasized a Pentagon scenario to the effect that our air strikes used "smart bombs," which were designed to hit only those targets that we intended to destroy. The clear impression was that we were waging a war in which no excessive damage nor superfluous human casualties were either intended or caused. "Collateral damage" was presumed minimal, unavoidable, and necessary. Two questions, however, remained unanswered. 1) Did we aim only at military targets? Were these targets militarily so important that civilian "collateral damage" could be justified? Obviously the bombs were only as smart as the bombardier who released them. 2) What was the proportion of "smart bombs" to "dumb bombs?" We have now learned that only 7 percent of the bombs were of the "smart" variety, while 93 percent were of the "dumb" kind. These "dumb" bombs had no more "intelligence" than to fall to the ground. B-52 bombers used "dumb bombs" exclusively, and B-52 carpet bombings were without discrimination. Considering this fact it would be naive to imagine that after about ninety-seven thousand aerial sorties where the bombs were not aimed, we wouldn't have killed at least some civilians. Current United Nations estimates list the casualties as 150,000 Iraqi soldiers, 20,000 of whom were slain after the "cease fire," while the troops were retreating in compliance with UN Resolution 660; 100,000 Iraqi civilians; and 385 Allied casualties, of whom 16 were US combat deaths. UNICEF calculated that the percentage of civilians killed or injured in all wars over the past ten years was about 84 percent. Thus the "collateral damage" to civilians was probably on a massive scale. It is difficult to assess how significant ninety-seven thousand sorties are until we note that this is sixty thousand more than were mounted against Japan during the last year of World War II.

If we imagined, incorrectly, that Resolution 678 did sanction military force to get Iraqi troops out of Kuwait, how could we explain the bombing of Iraqi cities? Such bombing policy had nothing to do with any of the Security Council resolutions. The military euphemism "denying the enemy an infrastructure" meant quite simply bombing water, fuel, food, electricity, medical, and transportation supplies for the civilian population. President Mitterand once warned the allies not to use weapons "whose use would mark a retreat into barbarity." One of the most common bombs used against Iraqi cities was the Rockeye Cluster Bomb (Mark 20), which is composed of twenty-four bomblets, each an antipersonnel grenade that explodes into two thousand high velocity needle sharp fragments that wipe out anything that stands or moves. These are hi-tech dumdums, of the kind prohibited by The Hague, Geneva, and United Nations resolutions. Nor were we told that the supposedly precise and "humanitarian" Tomahawk cruise missiles deliver three "packages" of "grenade submunitions" that spray tens of thousands of small pieces of shrapnel aimed at "soft targets," meaning people.

One of the myths inherited from the Vietnam War was that the United States fought that war with "one hand tied behind its back." If seven and a half million tons of bombs dropped on a rural land, and two and a half million, mostly civilian, casualties was a war of restraint, can we imagine what we must have done in Iraq, where we were told, as one pilot remarked, "we don't have the manacles on us this time."

Furthermore once the Iraqi troops began to evacuate Kuwait in compliance with UN Resolution 678, they had to pass through the US forces surrounding Kuwait. Common sense would have presumed that since the Iraqis were complying they should have been allowed to pass freely. This was not the case, and what followed was euphemistically called by the US troops a "turkey shoot." Such needless and unsanctioned slaughter had no United Nations backing at all. Even if the war had UN approval, it was not part of either military tradition or Resolution 660 that compliance would be followed by attack. Nothing in Resolutions 660 or 678 implied that this would be a war of "no quarter."

3. WERE NONCOMBATANTS SPARED?

We will not know the degree to which civilian casualties occurred until some agency more neutral than the United States counts the cost. What we do know is that both our weapons and our strategies entailed that we would be undiscriminating in our targets. Perhaps the UN Commission on Human Rights, the International Red Cross, the Red Crescent, or the Swedish Peace Institute will one day tally the civilians killed, wounded, or displaced. We know that there is still massive civilian suffering in

Kuwait and Iraq. We know that the Kurds and Palestinians face special persecution. A Harvard University report estimates that 3,000 civilian refugees are dying daily and that 170,000 will have perished by the end of this summer, 1991. Nine out of ten civilian casualties will have occurred after the cease fire. Such collateral damage is a shared US and Iraqi responsibility. Can such results be defended as proportional? In the absence of information it has been too easy to blame all such suffering on Saddam Hussein. Regardless of such pharisaical temptations, these are all casualties of the war waged by both sides, and both must share blame. Indeed the U.S. urged the Kurds and others to revolt against Saddam Hussein, revolts doomed to fail. Hence the responsibility for what is happening to these civilians after the war is a joint one.

None of these questions has an easy answer, but then "just war" claims are not easy ones to validate. Furthermore the indiscriminate havoc of this war needs a more compelling defense than the protection of oil resources, which has been the primary argument of our State Department ever since the start of the conflict. The claim that this was a war to defend Kuwait from Iraqi aggression is unpersuasive for just war theorists for at least two reasons. Kuwait is no more democratic than Iraq. It will be returned to the ruling al Sabah family, not to the Kuwaiti people. Furthermore if we are concerned about invaded lands, the Middle East has many cases for us to keep in mind. Hence the refusal to consider "linkage" during the early period from August through December does not support the claim, at this point, either that negotiations were carried out in earnest or that the war was waged to protect national integrity. Whatever claims one may wish to make concerning the gulf war, the just war claim cannot be defended.

NOTES

AUTHOR'S NOTE: This paper is dedicated to the memory of A. J. Muste (1885-1967), for fifty years a pioneer for peace through the Fellowship of Reconciliation. He persuaded me in the 1930s that all of us who believe in some kind of moral order face a crucial question as we face war. The question is not whether we might die in war. The question is "what moral price are we prepared to pay for our country's victory in war?"

1. This problem is discussed in Tucker 1960, p. 11.

2. These statistics are from the *Bulletin of Atomic Scientists* April 1964.

3. The trials are discussed in Knoll and McFadden 1970, Lozier 1961, Wright 1947, Minear 1971, Korovin 1946, and Taylor 1949.

REFERENCES

Davis, George B. 1980. "The Amelioration of the Rules of War on Land." *American Journal of International Law* 1 (January): 57-62.
Jackson, Robert H. 1946. *The Case Against the Nazi War Criminals*. New York: Alfred A. Knopf.
Kent, George. 1990. *War and Children's Survival*. Honolulu: Matsunaga Institute for Peace.
Knoll, Erwin and Judith Nies McFadden. 1970. *War Crimes and the American Conscience*. New York: Holt, Rinehart, and Winston.
Korovin, Eugene A. 1946. "The Second World War and International Law." *American Journal of International Law* 40, no. 4 (October):742-55.
Lozier, Marion E. 1961. "Nuremberg: A Reappraisal." *Columbia Journal of Transnational Law* I, II.
Minear, Richard H. 1971. *Victor's Justice: The Tokyo War Crimes Trial*. Princeton: Princeton University Press.
Oppenheim, L. 1952. *International Law: A Treatise*. London: Longmans.
Taylor, Telford. 1949. *Final Report to the Secretary of the Army on the Nuerenberg War Crimes Trials Under Control Council Law No. 10*. Washington, D.C.: U.S. Government Printing Office.
Tucker, Robert W. 1960. *The Just War*. Baltimore: Johns Hopkins.
Wright, Quincy. 1947. "The Nuerenberg Trial." *Journal of Criminal Law and Criminology* 37, no. 6 (March-April): 477-78.

Part II

The Gulf

We know that this is a just war, and we know that, God willing, this is a war we will win.

George Bush

We are being faithful to the values which God almighty has inspired in us.

Saddam Hussein

Engulfed in War: On the Ambivalence of the Just War Tradition during the Gulf Crisis

ROGER WILLIAMSON

Part 1: Was It Right To Go To War?

1.1. OBJECTIVES IN THE GULF CRISIS

The key objective in the crisis was to ensure that Iraq desisted from its occupation of Kuwait and committed no further acts of aggression; or to put it another way, to ensure that the relevant resolutions of the United Nations Security Council were made effective by concerted international action.

The expanded war objectives, expressed particularly by US politicians, were illegitimate. It was extraordinary that the possibility of Saddam Hussein withdrawing his troops from Kuwait and thereby fulfilling the UN resolutions was often referred to as the "nightmare scenario," because this would not allow the allies to "smash Saddam" or "render him incapable of further aggression." The latter objective, namely preventing further aggression in the region, continues to be a necessary and worthwhile goal, but, as will become clear in the following pages, it should be achieved by a comprehensive security arrangement for the entire region.

1.2. RELEVANT ARTICLES OF THE UNITED NATIONS CHARTER

Article 51

"Nothing in the present Charter shall impair the inherent right of individual or collective self-defence if an armed attack occurs against a Member of the United Nations, until the Security Council has taken measures necessary to maintain international peace and security. Measures taken by Members in the exercise of this right of self-defence shall be immediately reported to the Security Council and shall not in any way affect the authority and responsibility of the Security Council under the present Charter to take at any time such action as it deems necessary in order to maintain or restore international peace and security."

Article 41
"The Security Council may decide what measures not involving the use of armed force are to be employed to give effect to its decisions, and it may call upon the Members of the United Nations to apply such measures. These may include complete or partial interruption of economic relations and of rail, sea, air, postal, telegraphic, radio, and other means of communication, and the severance of diplomatic relations."

Article 42
"Should the Security Council consider that measures provided for in Article 41 would be inadequate or have proved to be inadequate, it may take such action by air, sea, or land forces as may be necessary to maintain or restore international peace and security. Such action may include demonstrations, blockade, and other operations by air, sea, or land forces of Members of the United Nations."

Subsequent paragraphs (Articles 43 and following) indicate the kind of military measures available to the UN should sanctions fail.

1.3. THE CRITERIA OF THE JUST WAR THEORY

1.3.1. The Just War Theory: Historical Background
Christianity began as a pacifist religion. The followers of Jesus modeled their life on his teaching, particularly the Sermon on the Mount (Matthew 5-7, Luke 6). Christianity also began as a religion of the poor and oppressed, but as it grew in numbers and influence within the Roman Empire, its social location changed. The major change occurred when Emperor Constantine made Christianity the state religion in the early fourth century, having seen a vision with the sign of the cross and the message "*in hoc signo vinces*" [you will conquer under this si_n] at the Battle of Milvian Bridge (Bainton 1960, 84-87). What happened would have been unimaginable for the earliest Christians, that "Caesar becomes a Christian and remains Caesar."[1] The change in Christianity's social

location was not simply one of reverting from consistent pacifism to readiness to engage in war, but a much more far-reaching one. The Constantinian transformation meant that Christians now took part in wars, in the administration of the empire, and in the execution of justice. In fact Christianity became the state religion, whereas previously it had only been tolerated or even persecuted.[2]

Under these new circumstances it became clear that a consistent body of teaching or a set of criteria was required to help to distinguish between wars that were permissible or even necessary and those that could not be justified. This was provided by St. Augustine and others (Johnson 1987, 328-29).

The intention of the just war theory was seriously corrupted, however. This is perhaps most clearly seen in the Middle Ages, the period of the Crusades, which were a deep perversion of the spirit of Christianity, using it as an ideology to attack others' religions (Bainton 1960, 101-21). Both Islam and Judaism suffered under this distorted and violent strain in Christianity.

1.3.2. The Just War Theory: Contemporary Understanding

A good summary of the criteria of the just war theory is given by the Rt. Revd. Richard Harries, now Bishop of Oxford, who is known as one of the most lucid advocates of deterrence based on the just war principles. He chaired the most recent Working Party of the Church of England on peace, defense, and security issues (Church of England 1988). Although differences in interpretation emerge in the detailed application and consequences drawn from them, Harries widely accepted version of the principles runs as follows:

The main conditions that must be fulfilled for a war to be just are:

1. It must be declared by supreme authority.
2. The cause must be just.
3. War must be a last resort. Every effort must have been made to resolve the crisis by peaceful means.
4. The expected war must not inflict more harm than would otherwise be suffered (the principle of proportion).
5. There must be a reasonable chance of success.
6. The war must be fought with the right intention. It must be waged with a view to establishing a just peace.

The two main moral conditions that must be observed in the conduct of the war (*ius in bello*) are as follows:

1. Noncombatants must not be the direct and intentional object of attack.

2. An attack on a particular target must be proportionate (Harries 1986, 64-65).

1.3.3. Comments on the Application of the Just War Criteria to the Gulf Crisis

1.3.3.1. Supreme Authority

In this instance the authority to be recognized was that of the United Nations. It is indeed encouraging to find virtual unanimity in condemning the unlawful annexation and invasion of Kuwait. There was good cause for concern, however, as it became increasingly clear that the UN resolutions were being used as the basis for a war led by the US over which the UN had virtually no control. The decision of the UN Security Council (Resolution 678) that opened the way for the use of force did not mean that war had to be automatic or immediate after midnight on January 15th. Other means could still have been tried to prevent the use of force being necessary.

1.3.3.2. Just Cause

It was clear that the annexation and invasion of Kuwait by Iraq contravened international law and constituted a just cause for war. Iraqi official sources contested this, but their understanding contravened the international consensus (Hussein 1990).

In the background of this issue, there is another major issue of political and historical significance affecting many parts of the world, namely the sanctity of boundaries drawn up by, as a result of, or after the involvement of colonial powers. There is much to be said for the realization that the past cannot be undone, but the acceptance of all inherited borders is itself also problematic. Certainly the principle that these borders should not be changed unilaterally by military force is one which should be upheld. Sydney Bailey, the Quaker UN expert, often cites the wisdom of the Organization of African Unity in their stance that unjust colonial borders should not be redrawn by warfare.

1.3.3.3. Last Resort

The term "last resort" means that all other reasonable means short of war must have been tried. There is thus a double sense to the word "last." In this instance it meant that other options must be taken. It further meant that sanctions should have been given a chance to take effect. In that regard the application made by former Archbishop of Canterbury Robert Runcie in a debate in the General Synod of the Church of England in November 1990 was admirable. The entire relevant passage on allowing sanctions time to work reads as follows:

> In saying this, I am conscious of the dilemma posed by the fact that after February major military operations become virtually impossible for some time. Nonetheless, the sanctions must be given some further months. A year of sanctions would be far cheaper in every way than even a very short war (Schwarz 1990, 4).

Sanctions would still have been in place and cumulatively working their debilitating effect on the Iraqi economy. Even though there was no guarantee, in the view of many experts, longer-term concerted use of sanctions could have achieved Iraq's withdrawal, thereby fulfilling the just war criteria concerning competent authority and last resort. What the archbishop proposed was prudent and a good application of the just war tradition.

Time magazine pointed out various arguments in favor of early military action, including the difficulty of holding the coalition together and the need to move before the hot season began in March, which is also the season of fasting and pilgrimage. In the words of one intelligence officer: "Ramadan is no time to have infidels killing Muslims" (Nelan 1990, 33).

The last quotation shows precisely the kind of logic that contravenes the careful reasoning of the last resort criterion. The weather and Ramadan are used as arguments to suggest that waiting six months is all that is possible under the last resort criterion. This is surely not the case and the proposal of Archbishop Runcie, namely to sit it out for an entire year, keeping up the diplomatic pressure the whole time, was surely a better application.

It is simply not true that one cannot have a large army, ready for battle at any time, waiting for more than six months. Obviously it is a problem to have a substantial army in such hot conditions for a year or more, but it would have been possible for them to be there and ready for war. That was the situation with NATO troops in Europe for over four decades. The argument for patience in waiting for sanctions to work was well expressed by military experts such as Admiral William Crowe and David C. Jones (retired Air Force

General), testifying before the US Senate Armed Services Committee (*Newsweek,* Dec. 10, 1990, 14). However, arguments such as those about the weather and Ramadan prevailed, and thus the military logic and political difficulties of maintaining the coalition helped the momentum towards war.

Clearly the continued suffering of Kuwait had to be a central consideration, but the damage that could be foreseen as a result of war also should have been more carefully weighed. During November and December 1990, the efficacy of sanctions as a sufficient lever to remove Saddam Hussein from Kuwait was increasingly questioned. This is ironic in view of their comprehensive effect, to which CIA director William Webster testified (*Guardian,* Dec. 17, 1990, 19). Most assessments conclude sanctions were being enforced effectively. Webster told the US Armed Services Committee that "more than 90 per cent of imports and 97 per cent of exports have been shut off. Although there is smuggling across Iraq's borders, it is extremely small relative to Iraq's pre-crisis trade" (Wintour 1991, 8).

Obviously sanctions could not have been expected to reduce the Iraqi economy to impotence within four months. Therefore it was regrettable that at a time when remarkably watertight sanctions had been imposed, US and British political leaders were decrying their effectiveness and saying that devastating war was the only alternative to total withdrawal. This cannot be said to have been a correct application of the last resort criterion.

The delegation of British church leaders which visited the Foreign Secretary, Douglas Hurd, on January 9th, 1991, made precisely this point:

> the delegation is deeply concerned that the implementation of sanctions, which initially received unprecedented international support, including that of the British and Irish Churches, appears to have been completely taken over by the military option and that military considerations have evidently taken precedence over all other possibilities, including diplomatic efforts. . . . Sanctions are not a soft option. They are intended to pressurize by coercion and there is evidence that they have been starting to take effect in Iraq itself.

In the light of this analysis, the British church leaders' delegation drew attention to the fact that the UN Security Council Resolution 678 does not specify January 15th as the date on which military action must inevitably begin, and it should not signal the end of efforts for a peaceful solution (Council of Churches 1991).

1.3.3.4. Reasonable Chance of Success

In order to assess the chances of success, it is necessary to know what the goals of any operation are. In this case, there were two main versions. One was to break Saddam Hussein and his war machine, as well as enforce his withdrawal from Kuwait. The other was to ensure his withdrawal and the enforcement of the UN Security Council resolutions. The latter goal is what the international community authorized and what should have been the goal--provided that the international community could be credibly assured and could take adequate precautions to ensure that no further aggression by Iraq should occur.

The difficulty was that one goal could phase into the other, and that the troops deployed could be used for either purpose. The Bishop of Manchester, speaking in the House of Lords, was not alone in worrying that the USA had much wider objectives than those authorized by the UN (*Guardian*, Feb. 7, 1991, 10).

The criterion concerning reasonable chance of success is important. Adequate strength in order to make this possible was required. There was a prima facie case after August 2 for a strong military presence in the region in order to press Saddam Hussein into agreeing to withdraw. This military force should have been there to enforce sanctions and to threaten use of military force as a last resort--really as a last resort.

Let us look for a moment at the criterion of "reasonable chance of success," given that the war option was taken by the US and its allies. The most important point is that even the predictable crushing military victory over Iraq by no means guarantees long-term peace and stability in the region.

At various times at least four distinct US policy goals emerged:

a) Enforcing Iraqi withdrawal from Kuwait and the implementation of the relevant UN Security Council resolutions.
b) Protection of Saudi Arabia and the prevention of further Iraqi aggression.
c) The destruction of the Iraqi "war machine" and ousting President Saddam Hussein.

d) Maintenance of a cheap supply of oil to the West, preventing Saddam Hussein from getting a "stranglehold" on oil supplies to the West, thereby causing catastrophic economic recession.[3]

For our purposes here, however, it is sufficient to distinguish between two variants: the liberation of Kuwait, and the destruction of Saddam Hussein's military power or regime itself. It is clear that commitment to the liberation of Kuwait did not necessarily require massive attacks on Iraq in order to achieve the destruction of Saddam Hussein's military capability. Clearly withdrawal and voluntary dismantling of the war machine would have been ideal. That, however, was always unlikely in the extreme! It was at least theoretically possible to imagine his enforced retreat without the bombing of Baghdad and the total destruction or surrender of the regime's military capacity. This would have had to have been accompanied by the containment of his military force or conditions for its complete or partial dismantling so as to satisfy fears about the recurrence of aggression. After all NATO (mainly the US) contained the Warsaw Pact in Europe without war for forty years, until the threat of Warsaw Pact aggression virtually dissolved. Surely the US military planners were not seriously arguing that Saddam Hussein was a more dangerous and powerful opponent than the accumulated might of the Warsaw Pact--about whose might and evil intentions they left no doubt during the various phases of the Cold War. Nonetheless military preparedness was able to contain that threat. If military containment, economic isolation, and political pressure were adequate against that far greater threat, why was this not felt to be sufficient in this case too?

The other approach (which was actually chosen)--namely breaking Iraq's military, political, and even industrial strength-- required a major air assault on Iraq itself. There was a certain amount of talk about "surgical strikes" (particularly by Henry Kissinger). It was obvious prior to the major air assaults that it would not be possible to break Iraq's military power with a minimum of casualties. The "surgical strike" against Libya failed to kill its target. As Samir al-Khalil, author of *The Republic of Fear,* says:

If Gadafy could not be taken out with surgical air strikes, Saddam certainly won't be either. The Iraqi President is bunkered down in one of the many underground bomb shelters kindly built for him by Western expertise in the 1980s. These were designed to withstand everything short of a direct nuclear hit (al-Khalil 1990, 64).

Surgical strikes were still advocated, however. Thus Robert Wright, a senior editor of *New Republic,* wrote:

Along every basic dimension--political, geographical, even moral--air strikes against military targets (surgical strikes, as they say) are preferable to an all-out air-and-ground war (Wright 1991, 19).

Israeli commentator Saul Zadka argued in the same vein, "In fact, however unpleasant it may be, a massive air attack on Iraq is the only way to break the deadlock and, more important, to avert a much worse confrontation in the near future." Later in this article he said: "A joint massive air attack could decide the outcome of the war in its first few hours" (Zadka 1991, 21).

The kind of military action required either had to be totally effective and prevent any possibility of Iraqi response, or be so vast and devastating as to break Saddam Hussein's morale. He was prepared to fight and sacrifice his people for nearly a decade against Iran and unlikely to do less when his very survival was threatened by the US and its allies.

A decapitating air strike might sound fine in theory--but if it were only, for example, even 90 percent effective, one faced reprisals. Prior to January 15th, I and others predicted the following as possible options to which Saddam Hussein would resort:

--Setting fire to oil fields with massive ecological consequences;[4]
--Use of chemical weapons, which he had already used against his own Kurdish citizens (Williams 1991, 3);
--Attacks on cities in Israel, even by missile;[5] and
--Terrorist attacks in Western capitals or on civilian planes (Norton-Taylor 1991, 3).

Not all came true, fortunately, but enough did to be very alarming. In short, a reasonable prognosis suggested that the military option of attacking centers of Iraqi power and decision-making would be massively costly, unless it was successful in a surprise attack. After Resolution 678, the "surprise attack" possibility faded considerably. From then on Saddam Hussein's troops would obviously have been on a permanent full alert. This being the case, the scale of the attack almost inevitably involved very substantial Iraqi civilian casualties.[6] (The question of attacking cities and its evaluation under the just war criteria is taken up in section 1.3.3.7 on noncombatant immunity.)

The conclusion one had to reach on the "reasonable success" criterion was that even if, as one assumed and as happened, US air superiority led to an allied military victory, any war was going to be a very costly exercise in terms of lives lost and in economic terms-- particularly as we now know the Iraqi economic base was destroyed, and the Iraqis succeeded in attacking oil fields and more particularly cities in the Middle East, with Israel as prime target.

The world's political leaders should have considered the following conundrum. If Saddam Hussein was as ruthless as they said, he was capable of very brutal military action. That being the case, it would have been better to try to avoid this occurring. The infallible surgical strike was a military fantasy, so nonmilitary approaches based on diplomacy--backed up by the threat of force-- would surely have been a better approach than boxing him into a corner with no alternatives except total humiliation or a bitter fight. If Saddam Hussein was not so wicked and dangerous as he was painted ("Hitler," the "Butcher of Baghdad," and "mad" have been three popular descriptions), it should have been possible to achieve the required results without drastic allied military action. In either case the answer was the same. If a positive outcome could have been achieved without war, all to the good. War should only have been a last resort and that stage had not been reached by January 15th, 1991.

1.3.3.5. Right Intention

Right intention also relates to goals. Serious analysis needs to be done on the selective way in which UN resolutions are applied. There are additional questions concerning Western policies and priorities. Obviously one cannot be exaggeratedly purist about this. States have interests; they are not benevolent societies for the impartial implementation of international law. Having said this, however, one does have to look critically at the oil dependency of the Western economies, the confused and often disgraceful Middle

East policies of the Western democracies, arms trading, and other issues.

However, even if all this is admitted, there is quite sufficient in the way of "right intention" for this particular criterion to be met, for the goal of forcing withdrawal from Kuwait. Similarly energetic implementation of other UN resolutions related to military interventions in the Middle East was and is required, if only for the sake of consistency. This should not be thought of as linkage. The Palestinian question needs a solution because it is a grave injustice. It urgently requires solution on its own merits. It would damage the standing of the Western world still more if some notion of "avoiding linkage" further delays the search for a solution to the Palestinian question and the implementation of the relevant UN resolutions (Security Council Resolution 242 and the resolutions which call for its implementation). To press for a solution to the Palestinian issue never was nor now would be to reward Saddam Hussein for aggression. It would achieve a greater consistency by the West in applying UN Security Council resolutions and would be a contribution to long-term political stability for the region.

. It is vital to challenge the major powers, including the USSR, about the double standards and inadequacies of their policies, particularly in view of their role as major suppliers of arms to Iraq. Full and impartial implementation of all UN Security Council resolutions and opposition to *all* occupation of land in the Middle East, rather than sole concentration on the Kuwait issue, is the way to indicate that the West is seriously concerned about international law and morality. Conversely it would have been wrong for the argument to be reversed. The past failure of the West to do anything effective about Palestine, Cyprus, and Lebanon rightly was not used as a reason to fail to implement UN Security Council resolutions concerning Iraq's withdrawal from Kuwait. The appropriateness of the methods of implementation is the point at issue.

1.3.3.6. Proportionality

The criterion of proportionality is notoriously difficult to apply. It is not instantly obvious what should be counted into the calculations. To give one example: was the issue under dispute the right to independence and self-determination of Kuwait, a state with a population of around two million people (of whom, incidentally, well over half were not Kuwaiti)? Or was the international community intent on sending a clear signal to all small countries that their rights will be equally vigorously protected? Once again political judgments will differ. If the latter is the case, then the claim of the US to be the protector of small nations and protector of the rights of those nations to sovereignty and independence, can be questioned, to say the very least. The Nicaraguans, with their recent experience of the US mining their waters and then refusing the jurisdiction of the International Court of Justice, could tell a very damaging story concerning US respect for international law and the independence and self-determination of small nations. When taken to the International Court of Justice for mining Nicaragua's harbors and supporting the Contras, the US eventually "decided to withdraw its recognition of the Court's compulsory jurisdiction in *all* legal disputes" (Goldblat and Millan 1986, 250).

The US has in the past often regarded international law as something of a one-way street--only to be observed when it accords with US policy. But the jurisdiction of international law should not be recognized only when it suits that policy. We will thus have to assume that we were only talking about the freedom and self-determination of the Kuwaitis and not the wider principle that international law must always be observed. The wider principle should of course be observed, but that does not accord with past US practice; US observance has been selective.

In this case what did proportionality mean with respect to Kuwait's sovereignty? This is a highly complex and rather invidious calculation to have to make. How can one calculate how many lives were worth sacrificing to restore the independence of Kuwait? Which lives does one count? The life of a person of any nationality is equal in value to the life of a person from another nation. That is required teaching in the Christian faith, based on the understanding of all people being made "in the image of God," and of modern Christian understandings of the importance of human rights. But in calculating military strategy, one generally only thinks of the losses to "*our*" side. If one accepts this basis for calculation, how many "allied" lives was it worth risking?

In this calculation the character and determination of the opponent also had to be taken into account. Saddam Hussein had already shown the minimal value that he attaches to the lives of his soldiers, in an awful eight year war against Iran which cost literally hundreds of thousands of lives. Dilip Hiro gives as a conservative estimate "over one million" killed and injured on both sides (Hiro 1990, 250).

It was not safe to assume that Saddam would be prepared to risk significantly less in this situation. Nor was it necessarily safe to assume that he would not use the most destructive weapons in his arsenal, as indeed he had threatened to do against Israel. A man who would use chemical weapons against his own citizens (Kurds in Iraq) could not be relied upon not to do so against foreign troops in a war or, for example, against Israel, if he felt seriously threatened militarily.

In such circumstances it was important to calculate carefully what one was getting into and how many lives one was prepared to risk and lose. In the Vietnam War, successive US governments blundered into deeper and deeper commitments. What were the tangible achievements that justified the loss of these lives (Tuchman 1985)?

Statements by President Bush by December indicated an awareness of this problem. The logical conclusion of his statements about the war not being "another Vietnam" suggested US preparation for a massive, sudden, and crushing onslaught of a kind likely to result in high Iraqi casualty figures (*Newsweek,* Dec. 12, 1990, 8-13). Bush also stated that "no price was too heavy to pay" to achieve Iraqi withdrawal (Tisdall 1991, 5). While this was effective as political rhetoric, it was clearly not a careful assessment of the value of the lives of his own American forces or a calculation of levels of destruction likely to be caused by a military victory. In short it was effective as a statement of his own or US determination to win, but it was not a morally responsible assessment of the value of human life.

Prior to January 15th, I expressed the view that a long-lasting war which led to even half the number of casualties of the Iran-Iraq War would not have been proportionate to the aim of removing Iraq from Kuwait--particularly since other means, such as the combination of sanctions and diplomacy, were available. It is difficult to quantify how many lives such a goal would have been worth. It sounds mercenary and calculating to ask this question, but the military planners *had* to ask it. It was not a theoretical issue of moral calculus. Wrong decisions could easily have cost the lives of thirty, fifty, or one hundred thousand soldiers in a "Vietnam in the desert." (Bush was aware of these fears, which is why he promised that it would not be another Vietnam--but, as I predicted, that required massive air strikes, high levels of Iraqi civilian casualties, and therefore contravened the criterion of noncombatant immunity.) If another way was available, then clearly tens, or even hundreds of thousands of dead were not justified. Those who prepared the military contingency plans had a heavy responsibility. One of the issues which they had to face was how many lives--in most cases, other people's lives--they thought it was worth risking for the freedom of Kuwait.

Leaving troops in place, enforcing sanctions for a year, and if possible forcing a settlement, would have been well worth it, even if very costly in financial terms. The prolonged suffering of the Kuwaitis in the additional period of occupation also had to be a factor in the calculations in the other direction--but then again, so did the likely number of casualties (including Kuwaitis) in any armed action to liberate Kuwait. This is not to downplay the atrocities committed in Kuwait, which have been attested to by that most reputable of sources, Amnesty International, whose care in checking and cross-checking data means that their published information almost certainly gives only a partial picture of the scale of the atrocities (Simmons 1990, 22). In short, Amnesty always errs on the side of caution.

1.3.3.7. Noncombatant Immunity

The wording adopted by Harries indicating that "noncombatants must not be the direct and intentional object of attack," addresses an area of particular importance. The age of aerial bombardment, from the First World War onwards, has made this criterion of the just war much more difficult to enforce effectively. Opinions divide: some feel that this shows the redundancy of the just war theory; many others feel that it shows precisely the *relevance* of the theory. If one cannot attack an opponent without massive destruction of civilian life, then the war cannot be just. Given modern weaponry and the destructive potential of even conventional weapons, attempting to justify extensive civilian deaths on the basis that they were unintended or accidental is simply not convincing.

True to their earlier analysis, the US Roman Catholic bishops have made noncombatant immunity a central point of concern in their response to the crisis.

> In addition to these criteria, there are others which govern the conduct of war. These principles include proportionality and discrimination; namely, the military means used must be commensurate with the evil to be overcome and must be directed at the aggressors, not innocent people. For example, the Second Vatican Council declared "any act of war aimed indiscriminately

at the destruction of entire cities or of extensive areas
along with their entire population is a crime against God
and man himself. It merits unequivocal and unhesitating
condemnation."[7]

It is reflections of this kind which caused (former) Archbishop
of Canterbury Runcie to warn against

romantic ideas of a surgical strike, of some supposedly
'clean' operation that will only kill and maim the armed
forces of both sides. We must face the bleak, horrible
fact that a war could not be confined to the professional
soldiers, airmen, and sailors (Schwarz 1990, 4).

The teaching on noncombatant immunity should not be pressed to
absurdity. The first civilian casualty does not automatically make a
war unjust. Runcie made this point in the same speech (Wroe 1990,
3).

I argued that a major attack on Baghdad or even heavy
fighting in built-up areas in Kuwait, whether or not they were
verbally described as attacks on military targets, could hardly be said
to fall within the spirit and intention of the just war criteria--even if
they could be forced into the letter of those criteria since
noncombatants were not "the direct and intentional object of attack."
This was a vitally important issue, and underlined the importance of
clarity in formulating the goals of the operation headed by the US.

As early as August 4, highly placed US officials and military
analysts linked to the government were making statements in the
press about the possibility or likelihood of massive US air attacks on
Iraqi cities. Phrases used included "carpet bombing Baghdad,"
"reducing Baghdad to rubble," and "leveling Baghdad," in reference
to a city of some three million people (Lumsdaine 1990, 5). *The
Guardian,* in November, painted the following grim scenario:

Pentagon planners claimed yesterday that by crowding
his troops closer together in Kuwait, Saddam would
have created a "target-rich environment." That is another
way of saying that conflict in the cramped territory of
Kuwait would now combine World War I slaughter with
World War II devastation. Quite apart from the dangers
of escalation elsewhere in the Middle East, a liberated

Kuwait would probably resemble Berlin in 1945. As
Chancellor Kohl said in Paris, one should "think of the
end, not the beginning, of the enterprise," before considering military action (*Guardian,* Nov. 21, 1990, 18).

In the euphoria after the war, it is important to realize that the
outcome in Kuwait itself could have been very much more costly.
The military can argue that this shows the wisdom and accuracy of
their choice of tactics. One can, however, plausibly argue that it
could all have been much worse--and that the low cost in allied
losses was bought at a high cost on the Iraqi side in the
bombardment.

1.4. EVALUATION:
INTERIM CONCLUSIONS AS OF JANUARY 15TH, 1991
Detailed application of the just war criteria yields the following
result:

I) The world community was right to respond, through the
United Nations, to the aggression which occurred, by demanding
Iraqi withdrawal and applying sanctions backed by the ultimate
threat of force.

II) Sanctions should have been allowed further time to work.
The proposal by then Archbishop of Canterbury Runcie in his
November 15, 1990, speech to the General Synod of the Church of
England that this should mean one year of sanctions deserved
support.

III) Military action really should have been a last resort after
all other means had failed. The criterion of proportionality is very
important for the assessment of military action. It should have ruled
out bombing major cities and set a serious question mark against any
major war because of the casualties, military and civilian, which
were involved.

This short overview and comments on the just war criteria
indicate that imposition of sanctions for a one-year period, with
further intense efforts at negotiation particularly by the United
Nations, would have been infinitely preferable to a war--even
though there was no guarantee of success.

A major war could still have been avoided in mid-January,
when the deadline expired. War should, even then, have been
regarded as a last resort.

The United Nations, not the US government, was the
legitimate authority for deciding that all other means had been

exhausted. It can be argued that Perez de Cuellar indicated that he saw no further UN possibilities. This resigned admission and the role of the UN secretary-general as a whole requires detailed examination. Even the January 15th deadline should not have seen the end of attempts to achieve a peaceful solution.

Sanctions should have been allowed to work for one year (unless Iraq were to engage in further aggression). Diplomatic solutions should still have been energetically sought by the UN secretary-general, UN Security Council, and any intermediaries which they accepted.

Optimally a solution should have been negotiated under international auspices or should have been a Middle Eastern solution. (If the former, it should have had substantial Middle Eastern input.) Such a solution should have paid attention to the situation in the whole of the Middle East, and also set out to remedy other long-standing wrongs and violations of international law: Israeli occupation of Palestine, occupation of Lebanon by Israel and Syria, and Turkish occupation of Northern Cyprus.

Even if after a year the international community had had to decide that military force was required, war goals should have required careful definition. It would still have been very difficult (perhaps even more difficult with greater Iraqi consolidation in Kuwait) to wage a war against such a well-armed and determined opponent within the criteria of the just war theory--particularly taking into account proportionality and noncombatant immunity.

Urgent attention must be given to the construction of a world order based on the United Nations and respect for international law. This should mean an end to the era of interventionism--including US interventionism. Military intervention, if it is ever sanctioned, should be sanctioned by the UN. Since the allied offensive, it has become clear that if war is sanctioned again in the name of the United Nations, the UN should not allow one nation to run the war its way, with the UN being marginalized and unable to have any say in the way in which war is waged on its behalf.

Any solution found should have been in the wider framework of comprehensive security for the Middle East, possibly similar to the Conference for Security and Cooperation in Europe framework. This would have to involve a solution for the situations of occupation; recognition of boundaries; guarantees for the existence of states, including a Palestinian state; arms control and disarmament agreements, particularly reversing the current trend of acquisition of nuclear, biological, and chemical weapons; a ban or very severe restriction on arms transfers to the area and respect for human rights, particularly the rights of minorities and freedom of expression. Such a solution would have to have the acceptance of the states in the region and should not be imposed from outside.

Part II: Assessing the Conduct of the War and Its Aftermath

2.1. JUST CONDUCT OF WAR?

The argument thus far has looked mainly at what is technically called *ius ad bellum,* or the assessment of whether it was justified to enter into war. In my judgment, the allies should have waited for sanctions to work for up to one year. In light of the judgment that it was wrong to go to war, it would be possible for me to argue that it is unnecessary to continue to consider the other part of the equation, namely *ius in bello,* concerning the moral evaluation of the actual conduct of the war. I still choose to consider the conduct of the war, because I believe that here too the moral tradition of the major strand of church teaching, which has not embraced absolute pacifism, has valuable points to make.

2.2. NIGHTMARE SCENARIOS

In the build-up to January 15th, much was made of the "nightmare scenario:" the fear of key US administration personnel that Saddam Hussein would push matters to the brink and then withdraw, leaving his military might intact for further military exploits. But is it not rather the case that military action itself has produced the nightmare scenario? Prior to January 15th appalling suffering was being inflicted on the Kuwaitis. But we must look dispassionately at the results of the war. The liberation of Kuwait has resulted in:

> --the death of an unknown number of civilians;
> --the death of an unknown number of soldiers, hundreds on the allied side and maybe hundreds of thousands on the Iraqi side, many of whom were actually retreating from the battle when they were killed;
> --the destruction of substantial parts of the infrastructure of both Kuwait and Iraq;
> --ecological devastation, first and foremost as a result of the oil fires begun by the Iraqi soldiers;

--the threat of major outbreaks of disease in Iraq as a result of the damage to sewage treatment equipment and water supplies; widely reported severe shortages of food, leading to a reassessment of the embargo on food imports (Rosen and Amr 1991, 12);

--Saddam Hussein, who is universally acknowledged as being guilty of massive human rights abuses, is still in power; and

--civil war has been unleashed, with disastrous consequences.

It is already clear that massive repression has been used against the Kurds in the north and that bloody battles were fought against the Shiites in the south. The rebel forces could well have assumed that the US, with its characterization of Saddam Hussein as another "Hitler," could have been expected to aid them and "finish the job" of getting rid of the current regime. President Bush's televised appeal (February 15th) to the Iraqi people to rise up and overthrow Saddam Hussein had received widespread publicity.

2.3. COUNTING THE COST AND RESPONSIBILITY

How should the cost of various alternative courses of action be weighed? During the conflict a regular theme of the US and its allies was the remarkably low cost of the action in terms of allied lives. It was emphasized over and over again that this would not be "another Vietnam." This should be interpreted as meaning two things above all: first that the war would not lead to major loss of US lives over a long period of military involvement, and second that a crushing military victory would be achieved. What counted to the US, British, and other allied governments was winning fast, overwhelmingly, and with minimum loss of their own personnel. As a result there was a massive bombardment of Baghdad and other civilian centers. The full extent of the damage is not known. Keeping casualties down on the allied side led to use of a military strategy which inflicted vast damage on the other side. In this way the shame of the "Vietnam syndrome" was allegedly lifted. What no one has yet plausibly explained is how the shame of one unjust war has been lifted by the "success" of another unjust war. (Perhaps the answer is obvious: winning is all--morality counts for little.)

The evaluation in terms of the just war criteria produces results different from the Western military calculations for one simple reason. According to the just war approach, the humanity of the enemy is fully recognized. The casualties on the other side should also be considered as part of the cost in weighing up whether or not the war was "worth it." The just war criteria are part of the European humanist tradition, but they make sense even without a specifically Christian anchoring. The central insight is that the life of an Iraqi conscript is as valuable as the life of a professional British soldier. This is virtually impossible to communicate to the readers of a tabloid newspaper like *The Sun,* to people who support "our boys" rather than seeing the human face of the enemy.

Once the life of the enemy is also taken into the calculus, matters look dramatically different. Bombing and killing retreating columns of Iraqi conscripts begins to look like unnecessary slaughter, rather than simply further underlining the superiority of the allies, for the simple reason that the lives of Iraqi conscripts count. This should even have been obvious to those who most virulently hate Saddam Hussein--perhaps even more so to them, since they stress that he is a dictator. The conscripts were compelled to fight for a dictator, to engage in military actions few of them (we can assume) would have chosen. Like the Argentine conscripts who took the Falkland Islands/Malvinas for the Argentine junta, they had good reason to hate the ruler who ordered the military adventure. Now they were being killed while retreating. If you do not count the lives of the enemy as being of particular moral significance, if you want a crushing victory, if you want to lift the shame of Vietnam and so on, this makes military and political sense. If you are assessing matters from the just war criteria, it seems more like an act of mass murder.

The killing of those actually leaving the battlefield would also be a particular offence to Muslims, since there are strict teachings against such actions involving unnecessary violence: "Muslim jurists generally agreed that war is to be waged in such a way as to utilize the least bloodshed and property damage as was necessary in order to achieve victory" (Abedi and Legenhausen 1986, 24).

Matters, however, are not necessarily that simple. One can plausibly argue that even retreating soldiers have a military significance. Those who retreat today can advance tomorrow. Those who were used to occupy Kuwait, on return home, can be used for the suppression of the Kurds. Once war has begun, these are the kind of calculations which have to be made and, seen rightly, such considerations underline the wisdom of the "last resort" criterion. If there are other ways of achieving a satisfactory result without recourse to war, they should be taken.

The complexity has a further dimension. It was quite possible to predict some of Saddam Hussein's reactions and at least some of the results of unleashing war. In *Just War in the Gulf?*, which was finalized prior to the allied offensive, I did just that, in these terms: If the situation is really desperate for Saddam Hussein, his contingency plans could include any or all of the following:

--Setting fire to oil fields, with massive ecological consequences;
--Use of chemical weapons, which he has already used against his own Kurdish citizens;
--Attacks on cities in Israel, even by missile; and
--Terrorist attacks in Western capitals or on civilian planes.

The point of citing the above is that it was quite obvious, in terms of the assessment of the ruthlessness of Saddam Hussein's character and the possibilities at his disposal, that at least *some* of the above would happen. If something can be anticipated with that degree of certainty, it can be argued that those who precipitate such a response share, to some degree, the moral responsibility for it occurring. I give two illustrations. A psychiatric nurse working with a disturbed patient will do everything in her or his power not to provoke a violent confrontation, and will use other means to find a way through the situation. Police dealing with armed people holding hostages do not immediately storm the building where the latter are holding out, even if the police have the personnel and technology to ensure that they will "win" in an armed confrontation.

In either case force is rightly used, if ever, only as a last resort. Other means of persuasion are employed, rather than provoking a violent scene, with the cost of death or injury to those involved or to bystanders. This is the case even if a verdict would be returned which runs, "Look how awful this person or these people are. Look what they did to innocent bystanders." Because it was known in advance that this is what they would be likely to do, in extremis, to innocent bystanders, extra care is taken not to provoke the onset of a violent confrontation. Defenders of the US and allied policy will argue that this is precisely what was done in going "the extra mile" for peace. This was not, in my view, a correct judgment, since the sanctions option could still have been continued.

One can look at the devastation of the oil fires and the other predictable responses by Saddam Hussein in one of two ways, thereby reaching diametrically opposed evaluations. One can say: "Look, we were right, he is a dangerous and appalling man. He is prepared to cause untold suffering, ecological damage, and so on." Such a line of argument leads to the conclusion, "We were therefore entitled to use drastic military measures against him because of the awful character of his regime and leadership."

On the other hand, one can argue the other way round--as I would want to do. "Because we can predict what he will do if attacked, leading to additional suffering, we must strive to find any other possible solution to the crisis." In such an evaluation, responsibility for the death and ecological damage still remains primarily that of Saddam Hussein, but (using the nurse and siege analogies) those who adopt strategies which cause additional, avoidable suffering are morally culpable *to some extent,* if other means could have been used, even if these means do not provide such a clear result as military victory. This line of argument is difficult to assess, and should not be pressed too far. Carried ad absurdum, it could be caricatured as arguing that the allies are responsible not only for what they did, but also for what Saddam Hussein did, because they provoked it. The case I am arguing is a much more circumscribed version, which argues that the predictable results of resort to military action correctly belong to the moral calculation of the decision to resort to military force. In this case, my own conclusion is that this then strengthens the importance of the "last resort" criterion and further strengthens the argument in favor of restraint and really exploring every other alternative to war-- in particular, sanctions backed up by the threat of force, diplomatic isolation, and political pressure.

There is a highly developed scholarly debate on the subject of "intention" and the moral evaluation of unintended consequences. This has played an important role in the debate on nuclear weapons. The key point of difference is whether threatening to do something, which it would clearly be wrong actually to do, partakes in the wrong of the deed itself, even if the threat actually deters the opponent and is therefore not carried out. In my view, it does and therefore to *threaten* to use nuclear weapons is wrong, albeit not as wrong as actually doing so.

The argument I am proposing is an extension of the debate concerning the principle of double effect, which dates back to Thomas Aquinas. I subscribe to the view that consequences that are clearly "foreseen" cannot be separated from "intention," to use the terminology of Richard Harries. One cannot bomb a military target in a civilian population center with highly destructive weaponry and then claim that civilian casualties were not "intended," if such casualties were unavoidable given the course of action and weaponry chosen. The argument concerning smart weapons capable of destroying military targets in civilian areas without any casualties is a different point. My difficulty with that is that in spite of impressive TV footage of weapons disappearing down ventilation shafts, this was not the usual type of destruction wrought. The use of "smart" weapons does not then prove that you can fight wars in cities in a way compatible with the just war criterion of discrimination.

But, it will be argued, it is clearly not the case that the allies "intended" that the oil wells should be set alight by Saddam Hussein.[8] Such intention as there was belonged to him or whoever took the decision to ignite the oil fields. Nonetheless I do not feel that one can absolve the allies of all moral responsibility for choosing a course of action that did indeed lead to that and other serious responses by Saddam Hussein, which were predicted and widely seen as very likely to occur in the event of Iraq facing military defeat.

A military strategist, like a chess player, must always be aware that his or her opponent can also make moves. This should lead to attempts to block the obvious moves, mitigate their consequences, and if they cannot be blocked and impose too high a cost, a decision should be made not to take the steps that lead predictably to that outcome. Similarly in the moral evaluation of the costs of various strategies, those formulating policy and strategy have a moral responsibility to counter as many of the obvious moves as possible. This is a complex area and debate will continue.

2.4. IS THE JUST WAR TEACHING HELPFUL IN PREVENTING OR LIMITING WAR?

It is my contention that the just war criteria, if properly applied, would perform their function of ruling out almost all wars, and would provide critical limitations to the conduct of war in the very few, exceptional cases remaining when the criteria of *ius ad bellum* were met. However, in practice, the conscientious application of the just war criteria has hardly ever, to my knowledge, prevented a major war. As Jim Wallis points out, "Every war in the history of this country has been called 'just' by the president who waged it" (Wallis 1991, 1). In Britain, too, the average consciousness is that all our wars, up to and including the Falklands and the Gulf Wars, have been just. Even if the mainstream churches are not enthusiastically in favor of war, the just war criteria have not proved a sharp enough stimulus to prevent those wars being waged. The problem is in their application, where political judgments, the use of the media, distorted perceptions as a result of socialization, the closeness of Church and State, and other factors play a role.

I thus come to an unsatisfactory conclusion. Not being an absolute pacifist, I see the need for the relatively complicated criteria of the just war theory. In almost all circumstances, conscientious application means that war with modern weaponry cannot fulfil the restrictive conditions that must be outlined. The theory itself and the criteria outlined provide a valuable moral framework for the assessment of the almost universal wrongness of going to war and the almost complete impossibility of waging modern warfare within these criteria. But usually the theory is misused to suggest that war is justified and can be justly conducted. This tells us more about the political misuse of the just war theory than its inherently unsatisfactory nature. It tells us, too, about the faulty judgment or political bias of those who, in applying the just war criteria, conclude that this or that war is justified. Often, too, there is simple misunderstanding or ignorance in the media, the general public, and sometimes from church spokespersons. A common misunderstanding is to think that the just war criteria only concern whether or not the cause for going to war is just (*ius ad bellum*), and the question of the morally defensible conduct of the war (*ius in bello*) is then ignored. In popular terms, this gives way to thinking along these lines: "We have now established that Saddam Hussein is evil, has broken international law, and so on. He now deserves all he gets." That is not just war thinking, that is justification of revenge.

I close this section with a parable on the ineffectiveness of the just war theory as a means of stopping wars. To my way of thinking, the just war theory is like an emergency brake on a train. The emergency brake should only be used if the alternative is crashing, or something similar. War, as a last resort, can only be used in extremis. The problem with the just war criteria is that they are regarded like "safety at work" regulations--which you have to have, which everybody ignores, but which have to be displayed so that the management can disclaim responsibility if anyone gets killed or injured. They are complicated and interfere with getting things done. In the case of the "emergency brake" on the train, if you make the conditions too complicated and comprehensive, you would crash while the driver was reading the conditions and trying to decide whether they apply. A set of emergency regulations as complicated as the just war theory and as open to interpretation would be of little help in deciding to use the emergency brake on a train. But each aspect of the just war criteria has its reasons and cannot simply be discarded to make things clearer. The way to simplify matters is for churches to say "No" to war, since the exceptions are so few and far between that they can be dealt with in the small print. Churches should now say that modern warfare is almost always incompatible with the just war criteria. The emergency brake should be taboo. All critical situations should be negotiated by other means.

This immediately raises the question: "What happens if the train is going to crash if we don't use the emergency brake?" The answer is: "Then you are driving too fast." If politicians continue to think: "Well, if all else fails, we can go to war," then wars will continue. If we rule out war as a means of solving international conflicts, nations will be less ready to supply dictators such as Saddam Hussein with weaponry, with credibility, with trading rights. I realize that my analogy only takes me part of the way to the "abolition of the institution of war," however, since I could not write that "modern warfare is *always* incompatible with the just war criteria." Honesty compelled me to write "almost always." So, taboo or not, I believe you need the emergency brake--but the Gulf War was a wrong application.

2.5. THE AFTERMATH: NON-INTERVENTION, THE KURDS AND THE JUST WAR CRITERIA

At the time of this writing (the first days of April 1991), the Kurds are being massacred. How is this to be assessed in terms of the just war criteria? Clearly it is appalling--but how is it related to the preceding events and an understanding of them based on the just war criteria? The US position seems to have been to create the conditions for a rebellion, to attack Iraq as long as Iraq was in Kuwait, but to do nothing tangible to stop the Kurds being massacred when they followed President Bush's explicit encouragement and rebelled. Suddenly, now this is a matter of Iraq's "internal affairs." If you never had a state or have been subjected for long enough, no one will help you. If you are invaded and have a state, like Kuwait, they may. (The discovery of oil may improve your chances, as in the case of Kuwait, or lead to that part of your territory being incorporated into another country, as in the Kurdish case with Iraq).

Sanctions, it is true, might or might not have convinced Saddam Hussein to leave Kuwait. There is no guarantee and no way of proving the issue either way. All that can be argued is that it would have been worth trying. One difference is that the application of sanctions would not have misled, or helped to push, the Kurds into a rising against Saddam Hussein, nor encouraged them into a course of action which has led to their slaughter. It is hard to argue that the imposition of sanctions would have given Saddam Hussein the pretext for the slaughter of thousands of Kurds. The war and the sense that "the time is now and the world is against Saddam Hussein" *did* lead to the rebellion and the murder of the Kurds. Who knows what would have happened within a year of sanctions? Saddam Hussein could have been ousted by a coup, by generals worried about the state of the economy. Someone could have shot him. Who knows?

What is certain is that since the end of military activity by the allies, Saddam Hussein has recovered sufficiently to crush the revolt of the Shiites in the south and to inflict heavy losses on the Kurds in the north. The Kurds are so frightened, with reason, that they have left their homes en masse. This has happened since the end of military activity, but, it could be argued, not necessarily because of US policy--*post hoc* but not necessarily *propter hoc*. *The Guardian* comments thus:

> The Kurds . . . rose against Saddam Hussein because they thought he was done for, because they felt they at last had the strength to control their own affairs--and because they thought George Bush was with them. The President of the United States called on the Iraqi people to rise against their oppressor. They did so. And now, it seems, he has left them to their fate. That fate is Saddam. And "he will kill, and kill, and kill."[9]

The Kurdish uprising was clearly a consequence of the war and, it seems plausible to argue, was a result, at least in part, of the call by President Bush for Iraqis to rise up against their oppressor.

Thus the known disastrous effects continue to accumulate. In the Shiite areas:

The collapse of the uprising in Iraq has led to the exodus of tens of thousands, if not hundreds of thousands, of refugees to US areas of control. The stream of refugees has drawn the Americans into what some officers fear could be an open-ended relief operation that will long outlive Operation Desert Storm (Block 1991, 13).

At the time of writing:

Hundreds of thousands of Kurdish refugees are desperate and freezing in the mountains along the Iraqi-Turkish border, trapped between the advancing fire of Saddam Hussein's armies and Turkish troops under orders not to let them cross. . . . Turkey made an urgent request last night for the UN Security Council to meet to discuss an emergency aid package to provide food, medicine and aid for the Kurds. "We cannot let them cross in. There are 250,000 of them," said Murat Sungar, the Turkish Foreign Ministry spokesman (Pope and Doyle 1991, 1).

The tragedy of this abortive uprising must also be seen as a consequence of the decision by the allies to use force. It must therefore also be included in the just war calculations of the cost of the war. This is not the place to go into detail, but it is also obvious that steps can be taken between total domination over Iraq and sitting back whilst the slaughter continues. Strict enforcement of the cease-fire conditions is one obvious point. While the Western governments begin to move with a humanitarian response, there are still political and moral questions to be resolved. Bush did call for an uprising. It happened and the US troops have stood by while a massacre occurred. John Major, stung by criticism, said in a televised comment: "I don't recall asking the Kurds to mount this particular insurrection." *The Guardian* (April 6, 1991, 22) found this remark "tart to the point of sarcasm, chillingly unfeeling, it was a jarringly inappropriate response to events the world has watched with grief and shame." The humanitarian aid promised is a welcome response to the immediate need. I would not want a further war against Iraq on behalf of the Kurds, since it would raise many of the same problems as the war to liberate Kuwait, but there are other possible responses, centering again around economic pressure, diplomatic efforts, and vigorous political condemnation. The

Kurdish catastrophe is a result of the war and at least in part, of US incitement to arms. The Western nations have a moral responsibility to help to achieve justice for the Kurds no less than they did for the Kuwaitis. In both cases war was not an appropriate instrument for the international community when sanctions, diplomacy, and political pressure were at hand.

Part III: Conclusion

This study has, at times, strayed from the careful dispassionate tone scholars usually adopt. If one were assessing battles far off in history, that would be one thing, but when the news of massacres is the daily accompaniment to breakfast, a measured scholarly tone is harder to achieve.

In considering the period prior to January 15th, the decision by the allies to engage in military action is assessed according to just war teaching. The decision whether or not to use military force (*ius ad bellum*) was weighed and the conclusion was that military imposition of sanctions was justified and that that course of action should have been continued, while political and diplomatic pressure was exerted. I added to this consideration some comments concerning the conduct of the war, which give cause for concern with respect to *ius in bello,* the just war criteria on the way in which war is waged. These included massacre of retreating troops, bombardment of population centers, and the complex point concerning the degree of responsibility the allies share for the predictable and vengeful response of Saddam Hussein. A full evaluation of the *ius in bello* phase cannot yet be conducted, since the full costs continue to mount and are not yet known. How many civilians and Iraqi conscripts did die? The most damning problem with the *ius in bello* criteria is that you can only know, in hindsight, on the basis of the toll in human life, whether a particular war failed to meet the criteria concerning conduct of the war. Also in considering the aftermath of the war, there too it is legitimate to insist that the costs of the suffering of the Iraqi civilian population-- through food and water shortages, destruction of the infrastructure, danger of disease, and suffering from reprisals after the uprisings by Shiites and Kurds (encouraged by President Bush)--are relevant costs to be included in the calculations.

A viable alternative policy, the extended use of sanctions, existed. Its success would not have been guaranteed and it would have meant the continuation of the suffering of the Kuwaitis under brutal occupation. But even the swift military victory has not been without cost to the Kuwaitis.

If the allies now consider that they have "won" the war on behalf of the Kuwaitis, at least in a narrow military sense, there are also many losers. The losers in this war include the Iraqi people (particularly the Kurds and the Shiites), the Palestinians, the Jordanians, and many others. The environment has suffered terribly, adding to the present and future human cost. My conclusion is thus that it was not a just war.

My secondary and less important conclusion is that the just war tradition and criteria continue to provide a valuable analytical tool for assessing such human crises, but have severe limitations as a means for preventing war, and, once war has been decided upon as the policy of government, have little impact in influencing the conduct of war. Careful analysis and judicious weighing of the criteria will not stop governments--only active campaigning that forms or changes public opinion can do that.

NOTES

AUTHOR'S NOTE: This paper began as an address to a seminar arranged by the Spark M. Matsunaga Institute for Peace of the University of Hawai'i at Mānoa on February 1, 1991. I am very grateful for the opportunity of speaking on that occasion. I would like to thank Rhoda Miller, associate director of the Institute for Peace, for her hospitality and the staff of the Institute for the invitation. I would further like to thank the Institute for providing the opportunity for publication of this expanded and updated study. I would also like to thank Louise Williamson for discussion of the content of the study and proof reading.

The bulk of this article, based on my study *Just War in the Gulf?* (Uppsala: Life and Peace Institute, 1991), follows the development of debate up to the expiry of the UN deadline of January 15, 1991. It was this section that formed the basis of my presentation at the University of Hawai'i. Those familiar with *Just War in the Gulf?* will recognize that this is an abridged version of the Life and Peace Institute publication. Sections two and three were added in light of subsequent events. Underlying this presentation are a number of my presentations on related topics. Throughout the developing crisis, my initial conviction has not changed: namely that sanctions (backed by military force to ensure their implementation) and diplomatic pressure, not war, would have been the most appropriate means for attempting to enforce Iraq's withdrawal from Kuwait and ensuring the full implementation of the relevant UN Security Council resolutions.

Every analysis has to stop somewhere. The latest information incorporated in this study was from the papers of April 6, 1991. This means that the proposal by British Prime Minister John Major for a safe haven for the Kurds could not be covered. It is a relief that some diplomatic initiative of such a kind is now being undertaken. The success of this proposal at the UN and even on the ground in Iraq remains very uncertain.

1. "Was für Tertullian undenkbar ist, das geschieht: Der Kaiser wird Christ *und* bleibt Kaiser." This quote is from Gollwitzer 1976, p. 130. Related material is found in Hornus 1980.

2. This is a rather shorthand and oversimplified account. Amir Hussain (WCRP Canada) pointed out to me that many Christians were involved in military service well before Constantine's time. He referred me to Adolf Harnack's classic *Militia Christi*. A helpful overview of the literature is found in Young 1989.

3. Ninan Koshy, director of the Churches' Commission on International Affairs of the World Council of Churches, gives a similar summary of the various formulations of US policy. I have expanded his version. Also see especially Van Elderen 1990, p. 12.

4. Varying estimates of the damage likely to be caused by setting fire to Kuwaiti oil fields are found in Brown 1990, which includes King Hussein's view of very grave consequences; a similarly serious estimate in Travis 1990; and in Butler 1991, an article by a British Petroleum plc managing director who argues that environmental consequences of oil fires in Kuwait have been exaggerated by other commentators.

5. See "Target Tel Aviv," in *The Evening Standard* (October 10, 1990), pp. 1-2; Flint 1990; and Fairhall 1990.

6. A more detailed assessment of military options and their cost was presented by Dr. Paul Rogers (Bradford University Peace Studies) at the ecumenical consultation (CCBI) organized by the British Churches on November 15, 1990. "Notes on the Consequences of a War" (unpublished).

7. "Letter to Secretary of State James Baker by Archbishop Roger Mahony, Chairman of the International Policy Committee of

the United States Conference," November 7, 1990 (duplicated), p. 3. Endorsed by the US Bishops' Conference, November 15, 1990; see the "Letter to The President by Archbishop Daniel Pilarczyk, President National Conference of Catholic Bishops," November 15, 1990 (duplicated).

    8. See Harries 1986, pp. 89-102, especially pp. 90-91; and Harries 1983, especially pp. 62-63.

    9. See the editorial, "A Glimpse Deep into the Quagmire," in *The Guardian* of April 3, 1991. The quotation within the passage cited is from the major article covering the entire front page, by reporter Martin Woollacott. A virtually identical wording is found in Morris 1991, p. 13.

REFERENCES

Abedi, M. and G. Legenhausen. 1986. "Introduction." in *Jihad and Shahadat: Struggle and Martyrdom in Islam.* Ed. M. Abedi and G. Legenhausen. 1-39. Houston: Institute for Research and Islamic Studies.

Bainton, R. H. 1960. *Christian Attitudes to War and Peace: A Historical Survey and Critical Re-evaluation.* Nashville: Abingdon.

Block, R. March 3, 1991. "US Stands by as Iraq Violates Ceasefire Line." *The Independent:*13.

Brown, P. November 7, 1990. "Gulf War 'Would Be Global Disaster.'" *The Guardian:*12.

Butler, B. January 11, 1991. "Putting a Stopper on the Doom-Gushers." *The Guardian:*29.

Church of England. 1988. *Peacemaking in a Nuclear Age: A Report of a Working Party of the Church of England.* London: Church House.

Council of Churches for Britain and Ireland. January 9, 1991. "Gulf Crisis: Church Delegation to the Foreign Secretary." Duplicated press release. London.

Fairhall, D. November 10, 1990. "'Stretched' Missile Could Hit Tel Aviv." *The Guardian:*8.

Flint, J. December 23, 1990. "Saddam Details Strike on Israel." *The Observer:*15.

Goldblat, J. and V. Millan. 1986. "Conflict and Conflict Resolution in Central America." In *Arms and Disarmament: SIPRI Findings*. Ed. M. Thee. 245-62. Oxford and New York: Oxford University Press.

Gollwitzer, H. 1976. "Zum Problem der Gewalt in der christlichen Ethik." In *Forderungen der Umkehr: Beiträge zur Theologie der Gesellschaft*. Ed. H. Gollwitzer. 126-46. Munich: Christian Kaiser.

Harries, R. 1983. "Nuclear Weapons: The General Synod Decision in the Light of Day." *Crucible* (April-June):58-63.

_____. 1986. *Christianity and War in a Nuclear Age*. London and Oxford: Mowbray.

Hiro, D. 1990. *The Longest War: The Iran-Iraq Military Conflict*. London: Paladin, Collins.

Hornus, J. M. 1980. *It Is Not Lawful For Me to Fight: Early Christian Attitudes Toward War, Violence, and the State*. Scottsdale, Pennsylvania, and Kitchener, Ontario: Herald.

Hussein, S. September 1990. *Message of Peace from Saddam Hussein, President of the Republic of Iraq, to the People of the United States of America*. Baghdad: Al-Hurriya.

Johnson, J. J. 1987. "Just War." In *A New Dictionary of Christian Ethics*. Ed. J. Macquarrie and J. Childress. 328-29. London: SCM.

al-Khalil, S. 1990. "Paying the Price for Saddam. In *The Gulf Crisis: The First Sixty Days*. Ed. The Guardian. London: The Guardian.

Lumsdaine, P. 1990. "Drawing a Line in the Quicksand." *The Fellowship* 56, no. 10-11:4-5.

Morris, H. April 3, 1991. "They Did Not Ask for Much." *The Independent:*13.

Nelan, B. W. November 12, 1990. "Ready for Action." *Time:* 28-33.

Norton-Taylor, R. January 11, 1991. "Anti-Saddam Coalition Steeled for International Retaliation." *The Guardian:*3.

Pope, H. and L. Doyle. April 3, 1991. "Fleeing Kurds Trapped at Border." *The Independent:*1

Rosen, J. and W. Amr. March 23, 1991. "UN to Ease Embargo and Let Food into Iraq." *The Guardian:*12.

Schwarz, W. November 16, 1990. "Runcie Pleads for More Time for Iraq." *The Guardian:*4.

Simmons, M. December 19, 1990. "Amnesty Documents Murder and Torture in Kuwait." *The Guardian:*22.

Tisdall, S. March 3, 1991. "'No Price too Heavy' for Securing Withdrawal." *The Guardian:*5.

Travis, A. December 27, 1990. "Dalyell Warns of Gulf Oil Infernos." *The Guardian.*

Tuchman. B. W. 1985. *The March of Folly: From Troy to Vietnam.* London: Abacus.

Van Elderen, M. 1990. "Gulf Crisis." *One World* (November): 11-15.

Wallis, J. February 1, 1991. "This War Cannot Be Justified." *Sojourners Press Release:*1.

Williams, N. January 11, 1991. "Soft Targets 'Vulnerable to Chemical Terrorism.'" *The Guardian:*3.

Williamson, R. 1991. *Just War in the Gulf.* Uppsala: Life and Peace Institute.

Wintour, P. January 9, 1991. "Sanctions Bite, But Do They Hurt?" *The Guardian:*8.

Wright, R. January 9, 1991. "Saddam: A Case for Surgery." *The Guardian:*19.

Wroe, M. November 16, 1990. "Runcie Urges Year's Trial for Sanctions Against Iraq." *The Independent:*3.

Young, F. 1989. "The Early Church: Military Service, War, and Peace." *Theology* 92 (November):491-503.

Zadka, S. January 11, 1991. "Ten Reasons to Strike and Preempt a Nightmare." *The Guardian:*21.

Ethics and War
in the Persian Gulf

MEREDITH L. KILGORE

IS THE UNITED STATES INTERVENTION in the Persian Gulf ethically justifiable? Some peace activists have stated guarded approval of the movement of military forces into the region, while hawkish conservatives have expressed misgivings. However, prior to an examination of ethical standards and their specific application to the gulf situation, the place of ethical discourse in determining foreign policy decisions commands consideration. The realist school of foreign policy studies endorses a tradition which assigns political leaders a different standard of conduct from that which binds individuals. This school has historical roots in the writings of Machiavelli and Hobbes and has been articulated by foreign affairs scholars such as Hans Morgenthau and Henry Kissinger.[1] To briefly state the realist argument, it is the duty of a head of state or representative body to pursue any action necessary for the defense of the state *and its vital interests*. This raises the problem of defining vital interests, but once that determination is made, the argument suggests that applicable means dictate actions.

National leaders appropriately take actions in the interests of the state that individuals cannot ethically undertake within society. Machiavelli went so far as to state that it is the prince's duty to learn not to be good; that a leader must resort to violence, deception, and perfidy to provide for the people under his authority. On Hobbes's account, commonwealths and their leaders exist in a state of nature with respect to one another and war, wherever possible, is inevitable due to human nature. The purpose of the state is to secure the life and well-being of the citizenry, and the leader who neglects to make this the first--or even sole--measure to guide political action fails in his function and breaches the trust placed in him.

The realist argument can and must be addressed on its own terms. A citizenry entrusts leaders to see that they are protected and that the necessities of life can be secured. The realist argument presumes that the moral and ethical norms of a society are lesser goods and are not vital to the life of the community, a questionable assumption at best. The mores of a society define the culture and the terms by which the community lives. Violating its precepts injures the fabric of society. Moral and ethical norms thus constitute goods in themselves not liable to expedient sacrifice.

War may be necessary in some contexts; determining what these contexts are and what the consequences of war are should involve careful deliberation. To regard ethics as sentiment, out of place in calm calculation of ends and means, distorts the essence of ethical discourse. Ethical acts are acts based on reason, and it is certainly not too extreme to hope that foreign policy will be determined in accord with reason.

However, the realist argument has the virtue of clarifying the role of ethics in foreign policy deliberation. There *is* an ethical obligation held by leaders qualitatively different from that which governs each of us in everyday social transactions. The leader of a nation is entrusted with the wealth and well-being of the polity. The virtue of individual self-sacrifice takes on a different aspect when that sacrifice involves goods held in common. An individual must eschew violence in most circumstances, but a head of state cannot renounce the use of force to the same extent. A different standard of behavior must apply, and ethical judgments rest on the basis of this other standard.

Such a standard is found in the just war theory. Just war criteria represent a lineage of thought stretching back to Cicero (Brodie 1973, 232). Acknowledgement that states face the necessity to wage war demands an added appreciation of the grave deliberations that the recourse to war requires. Just war theory is based on the premise that the purpose of war is to achieve a just peace.

The apparent contradiction of this premise is typical of the conceptual dissonance that arises when considering problems about war, as in the *para bellum* hypothesis.[2] Saint Augustine makes the argument that peace is the objective even of militant men; they do not pursue war for its own sake but for the peace they hope to establish in victory. Augustine takes this argument to its conclusion: a good ruler will wage only just wars and even then will do so "bewailing the necessity he is under" (*City of God* 19, ch. 7). Stating at the outset that the purpose of war is to achieve peace clarifies the terms of deliberation. This principle conforms to the Clausewitzian dictum defining war as a continuation of policy by other means.

The resort to war and the conduct of war must be firmly grounded in practical considerations. However, war threatens reason when conducted on an emotional basis. The fear and anger used to motivate a people during the course of hostilities tend to override rational considerations. Efforts to depersonalize the enemy for propaganda purposes end in uncontrolled polarization. During World War II the Japanese and Germans were depicted as less than human. In the current conflict President Bush compares Saddam Hussein to Hitler and the Iraqi president then responds with hyperbolic threats which harden anti-Arab stereotypes. Making peace with an enemy one has portrayed as demonic becomes problematic. It is the purpose of ethical discourse to maintain reason in the face of strong passions.

Just war criteria comprise two broad categories: *ius ad bellum,* outlining the just criteria for entering into war, and *ius in bello,* concerning conduct in the course of war.[3] Only three causes justify going to war: to protect the innocent, secure rights unjustly denied, or restore an order necessary for decent human existence. These requirements clarify Augustine's assertion that war is only just in response to aggression, by defining aggression as a violation of rights and good order.

The Persian Gulf conflict meets at least two of the conditions of *ius ad bellum.* The Iraqis invaded Kuwait and threatened Saudi Arabia and the other gulf states. The conditions that war can be undertaken to protect the innocent and secure rights wrongfully denied thus apply.

United States forces were initially positioned in Saudi Arabia for the express purpose of deterring war. Deterrence in the context of a just war theory has been addressed by the U.S. Catholic Bishops (1985, 139-146). The bishops conditionally endorse using even nuclear weapons *as deterrents* on the basis that they may prevent wars, both nuclear and conventional. In the Persian Gulf the United States and other nations assembled conventional forces to deter a war that could involve the use of weapons of mass destruction.

Any weakness of the bishops' position with respect to nuclear deterrence does not enter into consideration of the troop deployment to the Middle East. The threat to use force must imply that the actual use of force is acceptable. Willingness to apply force if deterrence fails is requisite for a credible threat. The bishops unequivocally oppose the use of nuclear weapons in any circumstances; this makes approval of their use for nuclear deterrence problematic. Similarly one cannot approve of the deployment of troops to deter war without also approving their active employment in extremis.

The third broad justification for resort to war, that of restoring an order necessary to decent human existence, applies to the gulf war as well. Narrowly, Iraq's invasion caused severe disruption and uncertainty not only in Kuwait but in the entire region. The threat that Iraq poses has resulted in the displacement of millions of workers from many parts of the world, seriously impacting the fragile economies of such nations as Egypt, Bangladesh, India, and the Philippines. This disruption has already caused suffering and holds the potential for much worse.

More broadly, a new global order is emerging in the wake of the Cold War where norms of conduct for nations, long given only lip service, begin to have real significance. The prospect for peace and development on a world scale is jeopardized to the extent that aggression is seen as a usable tool of statecraft.

Even when just cause for war exists, there are conditions that must be met prior to resort to war. Briefly war must be a last resort, preceded by the formal declaration of a lawful authority, and waged with just intentions. Furthermore war must be conducted in accord with principles of due proportion and discrimination, and a reasonable hope of success must exist.

Ongoing hostilities most clearly fit the last-resort criterion. An aggressor actively waging war leaves no opportunity for other methods to be applied. In World War II nations were attacked in the absence of serious attempts to negotiate differences. Where active hostilities do not exist or are suspended, other options short of war can and must be applied.

The United Nations has levied unprecedented sanctions in an effort to persuade Iraq to vacate Kuwait and enter into negotiations on outstanding disputes with the Kuwaiti government. Large forces have been deployed and it has been made clear that allied nations see a potential for war if Iraq does not respect the resolutions of the Security Council.

The requirement of last resort reasonably calls for sufficient time to elapse for Iraq to weigh its options and hopefully see a peaceful settlement as being in its own best interests. At the same time it is necessary to consider the plight of the Kuwaiti and foreign nationals under Iraqi control; they cannot be allowed to suffer abuse indefinitely.

In a war waged with just intentions the only legitimate objective is a just peace. Vengeance, greed, hatred, and ambition must be superseded by remorse at the need to use force. War cannot be used for conquest or economic gain. The most common criticism levied against the U.S. involvement has been the accusation that the conflict would constitute a war for oil. According to just war theory, material gain and the desire to secure resources are unacceptable reasons for war. This argument ignores the difference between seeking to secure a supply of cheap oil for the United States and assuring the free flow of oil to world markets. Oil is not an ordinary commodity but a basic resource needed to maintain modern economies. The cruelest effect of an artificial upsurge in the price of oil would be on the economies of less developed nations, where the means for meeting basic needs are already marginal.

This does raise a practical question concerning the effect of war on the world oil supply. It is the stated position of Iraq that it will destroy oil fields in response to any attack upon it.[4] If oil produced by the gulf states is cut off along with the production of Kuwait and Iraq, the result could be catastrophic. The determination of due proportion requires consideration of the capabilities and intentions of the enemy.

Emphasis must be placed and reiterated on the regret for the necessity of war. The Iraqi people need to be assured that conflict between governments does not imply animosity toward the Iraqi people and that there is no intention to destroy their nation.

A just war must be waged by a lawful authority. It requires the full authority of the state to bring the dangers of war upon its citizenry. Just war also requires a clear declaration setting forth the causes and aims of conflict. This declaration indicates to the enemy what conditions must be met to end the war. It informs other states of the relative justice of the war and demonstrates that the action taken has the full support of lawful authority.

For the United States, the president as the commander-in-chief of all military forces sent troops into Saudi Arabia, and obtained the support of the legislature in doing so. As long as the president proceeds according to U.S. law he acts as a competent authority. The authority of the nations in the region, especially Kuwait and Saudi Arabia, has been cited as well. Nations unable to defend themselves retain the right to ask for assistance in their defense. No forces from any country are in the gulf states without invitation.

Ultimately even higher authority has been invoked in this situation. In the past the highest authority has been sovereign states, but recently the United Nations has taken on new relevance. Prior to the initiation of any hostilities it would be proper and arguably necessary for United Nations authorization to be obtained. This would constitute the highest authorization for any war in history. A clear declaration of causes and aims has been made in resolutions passed by the UN Security Council in accord with article seven of the charter all states, including Iraq, agreed to conform to when joining. Security Council resolutions 660 through 667 specify what actions Iraq must take to satisfy the international community.

For the United States a declaration of war would be desirable to clarify U.S. aims to both the Iraqi and American peoples. In the United States an election has just passed without substantive debate on the prospect of a war that seems imminent. To the extent that the American people are not informed about the causes and aims of war legitimate authority is undermined.

A reasonable hope for success must be present for a war to be just. This condition marries ethics and practicality. While this appears to be an obvious consideration, it has been honored more in the breach; the majority of wars fought in the past two hundred years have failed to resolve the issues in dispute (Dunnigan and Martel 1987, 273). If there is no reasonable hope for success, then the recourse to war cannot be justified. Suicidal wars are unjust, even in the defense of high principles.

Clearly the nations aligned against Iraq could achieve victory over a single isolated nation. The calculation must take into account proportional means, but such means are available. Should Iraq launch an attack on Saudi Arabia it would be at a disadvantage. However, an attack by the United States and its allies on forces in Kuwait or in Iraq itself presents problems. These problems are best considered in light of the broad principles of proportionality and discrimination.

Due proportion means that the good to be done must outweigh the harm anticipated in war. Proportion must be considered both overall and in the specific means by which war is executed. Even in the context of a just war, specific military means to particular objectives may be disproportionate. The decision to use strategic bombing against cities or putting numbers of innocent individuals at risk must be weighed against the direct military objective being sought.

Even if the broad conditions constituting a just war are met, it is still necessary to consider the particulars. It has been argued that it would not be enough, for example, for the Iraqis to withdraw from most of Kuwait but remain in possession of one strategic and uninhabited island, and that the United States in that case should resort to war if necessary. However, it is difficult to justify the loss of life to be inflicted on Iraqis, Americans, Kuwaitis, and others when a small amount of disputed territory is all that weighs against it. Continued deterrence, economic sanctions, and other measures short of war would be appropriate, but large-scale loss of life would not.

The costs to be considered include the harm inflicted by allied forces against Iraqis, Kuwaitis, and the hostages being held within Iraq, as well as the harm that results from Iraqi actions. Leaders take on responsibility both for their own actions and for the consequences of those actions. Estimates of casualties vary with the type of action undertaken. If discrete assaults on military targets removed from population centers can be made, a relatively small loss of life would result. On the other hand, if Iraq responds with a large-scale war on Saudi Arabia and the allied forces using chemical and biological weapons, the results could be much worse. Estimates have reached fifty thousand American casualties with fifteen thousand dead, and two hundred thousand Iraqi military and civilian casualties. If Iraq strikes at Israel, as it has threatened to do, it could trigger a nuclear response. The casualties in such a scenario are incalculable.

Consideration of due proportion requires a clear knowledge of the capabilities of each side. There must be a high probability that the Iraqi ability to cause a total war in the Middle East can be eliminated. Iraqi missiles pose the greatest threat. Their modified Scud missiles have the capability of delivering chemical and biological warheads throughout the region, including Israel. But this type of liquid-fueled weapon requires preparations for launch that can be monitored, and the launchers are vulnerable to numerous weapons in the U.S. arsenal.[5] However, if the Iraqis possess SS-12 missiles, banned in Europe by the INF treaty, this presents a worse threat. The SS-12 is a solid-fueled, mobile, and concealable weapon that would be more difficult to eliminate than the Scuds. U.S. intelligence capabilities in the Middle East are quite good and the ability to destroy these systems seems probable. However, the degree of certainty required must be high for war to be a reasonable option.

The principle of discrimination complements that of proportionality; no intentional attack may be made against noncombatants and nonmilitary targets. This precludes the use of weapons of mass destruction and limits the use of conventional military means where an impact on noncombatants cannot be avoided. Even in the case of combatants, discrimination restricts the use of force against those who surrender their arms and seek quarter. In ceasing to participate actively in the war a soldier takes on the status of a noncombatant and may not be killed or mistreated.

The onset of war does not set aside all ethical norms; not all means are justifiable. The calculation of military exigency must take into account acceptable means of conducting war, but these constraints are not without some utility in themselves. Considerations based on ethical principles have been demonstrated to have military utility as well. When prisoners are well treated and their basic needs are met, there is greater incentive for them to cease their hostilities and surrender. The control of men under arms in preventing wanton injury to civilians and prisoners of war improves the overall discipline of a fighting force and allows the maintenance of a moral posture.

The greatest benefit of the restraint following from consideration of proportion and discrimination is seen in the light of the ultimate end of war, peace. Restraint and compassion in the course of combat will serve the difficult process of ending hostilities and agreeing to a new peace.

Two dilemmas arise with respect to the principle of discrimination in the context of modern warfare. Modern weapons often cannot avoid some harm to innocent people close to military targets. If taken as a total injunction against killing or injuring noncombatants, this principle becomes an absolute prohibition against the use of force, precluding any concept of just war. Similarly the distinction between combatants and noncombatants becomes increasingly vague in modern industrial states. Production and transportation centers crucial to the enemy's war effort can be vital military targets, and the workers employed compromise their noncombatant status by participating in wartime industry.

These problems allow three possible solutions: the rejection of just war theory, modification of its principles, or the rejection of war. The rejection of war implies that no use of force can be opposed by force in any circumstances. The rejection of just war theory leaves no clear standard with which to evaluate the proper use of force in particular circumstances. Modifying the discrimination principle allows the remainder of the criteria to stand.

The introduction of proportionality into concepts of discrimination serves to some degree to resolve these dilemmas. Terror bombing with no clear military utility is precluded, as is indiscriminate abuse of civilians by occupying forces. An injunction to minimize noncombatant casualties results, but the degree to which noncombatants present at vital military targets are protected remains vague.

The United States has invested billions of dollars in increasing the accuracy and discrimination of its weaponry. If this investment has indeed been made properly it should be possible to inflict severe military damage on Iraqi forces and at the same time minimize noncombatant casualties.

Should Iraqi forces attack the forces arrayed against them or if it is determined that adequate time has been given for other methods to work, war could be considered. In fact, if it is determined that greater good can be accomplished or greater evil avoided, recourse to war becomes a moral obligation.

In sum, the *ius ad bellum* criteria have been or can be met in the gulf if the nations involved are sufficiently interested in making an effort to do so. More clarity should be given to the presence of other, unstated objectives. A war for the sole purpose of preempting future Iraqi recourse to nuclear weapons would be unjustified; just war theory forbids preemptive wars. Further it has not been demonstrated that every other avenue of denying Iraq access to nuclear weapons technology has been tried and exhausted. The contrary seems to be the case, with Iraq having had considerable assistance from Western nations, the United States included.

Force can be more judiciously applied when other sanctions are applied concurrently. Strikes at military targets can be made contingent on the behavior of Iraqi forces occupying Kuwait. The use of military force could be suspended if neutral organizations were granted access to Kuwait to monitor and report on compliance to international human rights norms.

All of these principles and conditions have the effect of promoting deliberation prior to and in the course of engaging in warfare with another state. These are all necessary conditions; they must all be met. At the same time they are sufficient conditions;

when they are all met war becomes an imperative. If one is in a position to protect the innocent, secure just rights, and promote needed order, and all options short of war have been tried and exhausted, there is a moral choice to be made. To fail to intervene when one has the capacity to do so is to cede success to injustice. Just war theory is a two-edged sword; it restrains war in certain circumstances but mandates it in others.

Application of the principles of discrimination and proportionality requires difficult deliberation. There is an emerging world order in which this type of deliberation is increasingly possible. A decrease in the intensity of ideological conflict between the superpower blocs holds out the hope that greater reason will be applied to questions of foreign intervention, but such consideration requires continuous thought and attention. It remains to be seen if national leaders and their public constituents will be able and willing to realize the hope for an improved world order.

Postscript on the Gulf War--June 1991

The foregoing essay was written in November 1990, prior to the passage of Security Council Resolution 678 and its subsequent ratification by the United States Congress. In keeping with the dictates of this volume, I have decided to retain the essay as written, rather than to update it in light of unfolding events. This approach preserves a perspective which reflects an ignorance of outcomes, this state of unknowing being a necessary aspect of any discourse concerning a prospective decision to go to war. However, failure to comment on the course of the war that did take place would abdicate a responsibility to address the central thesis of this essay--that the just war criteria constitute a necessary and workable paradigm for the evaluation of questions of war and peace.

To begin, the war did not begin on January 15, 1991, and it has not yet ended. A blockade imposed by military means constitutes an act of war; a blockade was officially imposed on Iraq on August 25, 1990, with the passage of Security Council Resolution 665. That blockade remains in place at the time of this writing, and the cease-fire that came into effect with Resolution 687 defines the terms upon which peace may be concluded. Referring to the blockade by the euphemism "sanctions" is as gross a distortion of reality as referring to killing civilians as "collateral damage."

Those critics of the Bush administration's prosecution of the war who nevertheless conceded the necessity to intervene against

Iraq frequently iterated that the "sanctions" must be given time to work. A definition of "sanctions" broad enough to include a blockade needs little more breadth to include bombing and invasion as well. An extended blockade would have been as unacceptable from the standpoint of the just war criteria as indiscriminate bombing. The victims of such a blockade would have been those most protected under the principle of discrimination--the people of Kuwait and the weakest and most marginal elements of the population in Iraq. No argument that I have heard against the escalation of force, hinged on the "last resort" criterion, has adequately addressed the indiscrimination of a blockade.

Perhaps the most troublesome aspect of the war was the strategic bombing campaign carried out against Iraq. A long-cherished doctrine of the United States Air Force has related to the use of "air power." According to this doctrine, the proper use of air forces is to carry the war to the enemy's homeland and thus destroy his capability and will to resist. Numerous analysts during the course of the campaign commented that if air power alone could ever win a war it would do so in Iraq. Impressive technology added to complete "air supremacy" in favorable terrain provided an unprecedented and probably irreplicable advantage to the allied air forces. Despite these conditions the strategic air campaign, as distinct from the battlefield destruction and interdiction, failed in its mission to force an Iraqi withdrawal from Kuwait.

Two of the just war criteria militate against the use of strategic bombing: due proportion and *a reasonable hope of success*. If this lesson is learned, some good can be salvaged from the destruction pointlessly wreaked on Iraq. Worst case predictions suggest that more people, including children, could die of disease due to the destruction of public health and sanitation facilities in Iraq than there were soldiers killed in battle. It remains to be seen what the ultimate costs will be, but no military objective has been put forward proportionate to the destruction done. No strategic bombing campaign has been proven a success, not in World War II, not in Korea or Vietnam, and now not in Iraq.[6] The very flawlessness of the strategic bombing campaign, its truly "surgical" strikes, freedom from operational restraint and impeccable intelligence, viewed in the light of its lack of success, should write finis to the "air power" doctrine.

Another valid criticism of the war concerns the lack of foresight and subsequent paralysis of the coalition in the face of the

Kurdish and Shiite uprisings after the cease-fire went into effect. This issue was also not addressed in my original essay. The initial coalition reaction--inaction--indicates both a serious failure of intelligence and an abdication of ethical principle in favor of realpolitik. The present policy of establishing secure enclaves demonstrates the availability of options: if this or some other policy had been put in place concurrent with the popular uprisings, much harm could possibly have been averted. The fact that the United States and the United Nations were finally forced to act testifies to the unreality of "realism." Ethical considerations will not lie dormant if ignored.

NOTES

1. See, for example, Morgenthau 1973 (3 and passim) and Kissinger's essay, "The Moral Foundations of Foreign Policy" (Kissinger 1977, 195-214).
2. Discussion of the *Si vis pacem, para bellum* [If you want peace, prepare for war] theory is found in Luttwak 1987.
3. Discussions of just war criteria are found in Potter 1973, O'Brien 1985, and Payne and Payne 1987.
4. This position was stated by, for example, the then Iraqi ambassador to the United States, Tariq Aziz, on the Cable News Network, "CNN News Hour," November 10, 1990.
5. This discussion of armament is based on Cochran et al. 1989, pp. 215 and 220. The rumor of SS-12 presence in Iraq was reported on the Cable News Network, "Evans and Novak," November 10, 1990.
6. Strategic bombing campaigns are analyzed in the *United States Strategic Bombing Survey,* Momyer 1978, and Gibson 1988.

REFERENCES

Brodie, Bernard. 1973. *War and Politics.* New York: Macmillan.
Cochran, Thomas, William Arkin, Robert Norris, and Jeffrey
        Sands. 1989. *Nuclear Weapons Databook* 4. New York:
        Harper and Row.

Dunnigan, James F. and William Martel. 1987. *How to Stop a War*. New York: Doubleday.

Gibson, James, W. 1988. *The Perfect War*. New York: Random House.

Kissinger, Henry. 1977. *American Foreign Policy*. 3d edition. New York: W. W. Norton.

Luttwak, Edward. 1987. *Strategy: The Logic of War and Peace*. Cambridge: Harvard University Press.

Momyer, General William W. 1978. *Air Power in Three Wars*. Washington, D.C.: U.S. Government Printing Office.

Morgenthau, Hans. 1973. *Politics Among Nations*. New York: Alfred A. Knopf.

O'Brien, William. 1985. "Just-War Theory." In Sterba. 30-44.

Payne, Keith and Karl Payne. 1987. *A Just Defense*. Portland, Oregon: Multnomah.

Potter, Ralph B. 1973. "The Moral Logic of War." In *Peace and War*. Ed. Charles Beitz and Theodore Herman. 7-16. San Francisco: W. H. Freeman.

Sterba, James. 1985. *The Ethics of War and Nuclear Deterrence*. Belmont, California: Wadsworth.

U.S. Catholic Bishops. 1985. "On the Use of Nuclear Weapons and Nuclear Deterrence." In Sterba. 139-146.

United States Strategic Bombing Survey. Washington, D.C.: U.S. Government Printing Office.

Part III

The Last Word

There has never been a good war or a bad peace.
Benjamin Franklin

Metaphor and War:
The Metaphor System Used
to Justify War in the Gulf

GEORGE LAKOFF

METAPHORS CAN KILL. The discourse over whether we should go to war in the Persian Gulf is a panorama of metaphor. Secretary of State James Baker sees Saddam Hussein as "sitting on our economic lifeline." President Bush sees him as having a "stranglehold" on our economy. General Schwarzkopf characterizes the occupation of Kuwait as an ongoing "rape." President Bush says that the United States is in the gulf to "protect freedom, protect our future, and protect the innocent," and that we must "push Saddam Hussein back." Saddam is seen as Hitler.

It is vital, literally vital, to understand just what role metaphorical thought is playing in bringing us to the brink of war. Metaphorical thought, in itself, is neither good nor bad; it is simply commonplace and inescapable. Abstractions and enormously complex situations are routinely understood via metaphor. Indeed there is an extensive, and mostly unconscious, system of metaphor that we use automatically and unreflectively to understand complexities and abstractions. Part of this system is devoted to understanding international relations and war. We now know enough about this system to have an idea of how it functions.

The metaphorical understanding of a situation functions in two parts. First there is a widespread, relatively fixed set of metaphors that structure how we think. For example a decision to go to war might be seen as a form of cost-benefit analysis, where war is justified when the costs of going to war are less than the costs of not going to war. Second there is a set of metaphorical definitions that allow one to apply such a metaphor to a particular situation. For the cost-benefit metaphor there must be a definition of "cost," including means of comparing relative "costs."

The use of a metaphor with a set of definitions becomes pernicious when it hides realities in a harmful way. It is important to distinguish what is metaphorical from what is not. Pain, dismemberment, death, starvation, and the death and injury of loved ones are not metaphorical. They are real and in a war they could afflict tens, perhaps hundreds of thousands, of real human beings, whether Iraqi, Kuwaiti, or American.

War as Politics and Politics as Business

Military and international relations strategists do use metaphors of cost-benefit analysis. They arise through a metaphor that is taken as definitional by most strategic thinkers in the area of international politics--Karl von Clausewitz's metaphor:

War is politics pursued by other means.

Von Clausewitz was a Prussian general who perceived war in terms of political cost-benefit analysis. On his account each nation state has political objectives, and war may best serve those objectives. The political "gains" are to be weighed against acceptable "costs." When the costs of war exceed the political gains, the war should cease.

There is another metaphor implicit here:

Politics is business,

where efficient political management is seen as akin to efficient business management. As in a well-run business, a well-run government should keep a careful tally of costs and gains. This metaphor for characterizing politics, together with Clausewitz's metaphor, makes war a matter of cost-benefit analysis: defining beneficial "objectives," tallying the "costs," and deciding whether achieving the objectives is "worth" the costs. The *New York Times* on November 12, 1990, ran a front page story announcing that "a national debate has begun as to whether the United States should go to war in the Persian Gulf." The *Times* described the debate as defined by what I have called Clausewitz's metaphor (though it described the metaphor as literal), and then raised the question, "What then is the nation's political object in the gulf and what level of sacrifice is it worth?" The "debate" was not over whether Clausewitz's metaphor was appropriate, but only over how various analysts calculated the relative gains and losses. The same has been true of the hearings of the Senate Foreign Relations Committee, where Clausewitz's metaphor provides the framework within which most discussion has taken place.

The broad acceptance of Clausewitz's metaphor raises vital questions. What exactly makes it a metaphor rather than literal truth? Why does it seem so natural to foreign policy experts? How does it fit into the overall metaphor system for understanding foreign relations and war? And most importantly, what realities does it hide? To answer these questions let us turn to the system of metaphorical thought most commonly used by the general public in comprehending international politics. What follows is a two-part discussion of the role of metaphorical reasoning about the gulf crisis. The first part lays out the central metaphor systems used in reasoning about the crisis, both the system used by foreign policy experts and the system used by the public at large. The second part discusses how these systems have been applied to the Persian Gulf.

The Metaphor Systems

A. THE STATE-AS-PERSON SYSTEM

In this system the state is conceptualized as a person, engaging in social relations within a world community. Its landmass is its home. It lives in a neighborhood and has neighbors, friends, and enemies. States are seen as having inherent dispositions: they can be peaceful or aggressive, responsible or irresponsible, industrious or lazy.

The well-being or health of the state is its wealth. The general well-being of a state is understood in economic terms--its economic health. A serious threat to economic health can thus be seen as a death threat. To the extent that a nation's economy depends on foreign oil, that oil supply becomes a "lifeline" (reinforced by the image of an oil pipeline).

Strength for the state is military strength.

Maturity for the person-state is industrialization. Nonindustrialized nations are "underdeveloped," with industrialization as a natural state to be reached. Third World nations are thus immature children, to be taught how to develop properly or be disciplined if they get out of line. Nations that fail to industrialize at a rate considered normal are seen as akin to retarded children and judged as "backward" nations.

Rationality in this system is the maximization of self-interest.

There is an implicit logic to the use of these metaphors. Since it is in the interest of every person to be as strong and healthy as possible, a rational state seeks to maximize wealth and military might. Thus violence can further self-interest. It can be stopped in three ways: by a balance of power, so that no one in a neighborhood is strong enough to threaten anyone else; by the use of collective persuasion by the community to make violence counter to self-interest; or by a cop strong enough to deter violence or punish it. The cop should act morally, in the community's interest, and with the sanction of the community as a whole.

Morality in this metaphor is a matter of accounting, of keeping the moral books balanced. A wrongdoer incurs a debt and must be made to pay. The moral books can be balanced by a return to the situation prior to the wrongdoing, by giving back what has been taken, by recompense, or by punishment. Justice is the balancing of the moral books. War in this metaphor is a fight between two people, a form of hand-to-hand combat. Thus the United States might seek to "push Iraq back out of Kuwait" or "deal the enemy a heavy blow" or "deliver a knockout punch." A just war is thus a form of combat for the purpose of settling moral accounts. The most common form of discourse in the West where there is combat to settle moral accounts is the classic fairy tale. When people are replaced by states in such a fairy tale, what results is a scenario for a just war.

B. THE FAIRY TALE OF THE JUST WAR

Cast of characters: a villain, a victim, and a hero. The victim and the hero may be the same person. The scenario: a crime is committed by the villain against an innocent victim (typically an assault, theft, or kidnapping). The offense occurs due to an imbalance of power and creates a moral imbalance. The hero makes sacrifices and undergoes difficulties, typically making an arduous journey, sometimes across the sea to treacherous terrain. The villain is inherently evil, perhaps even a monster, and thus reasoning with him is out of the question. The hero is left with no choice but to engage the villain in battle. The hero defeats the villain and rescues the victim. The moral balance is restored. Victory is achieved. The hero, who always acts honorably, has proved his manhood and achieved glory. The sacrifice was worthwhile. The hero receives acclaim, along with the gratitude of the victim and the community.

The fairy tale has an asymmetry built into it. The hero is moral and courageous, while the villain is amoral and vicious. The hero is rational, but though the villain may be cunning and calculating, he cannot be reasoned with. Heroes thus cannot negotiate with villains; they must defeat them. The enemy-as-demon metaphor arises as a consequence of the fact that we understand what a just war is in terms of this fairy tale. The most natural way to justify a war on moral grounds is to fit this fairy tale structure to a given situation. This is done by metaphorical definition, that is, by answering the questions: Who is the victim? Who is the villain? Who is the hero? What is the crime? What counts as victory? Each set of answers provides a different filled-out scenario.

As the gulf crisis developed, President Bush tried to justify going to war by the use of such a scenario. At first he could not get his story straight. What happened was that he was using two different sets of metaphorical definitions, which resulted in two different scenarios: the rescue scenario--Iraq is the villain, the U.S. is the hero, Kuwait is the victim, and the crime is kidnap and rape; and the self-defense scenario--Iraq is the villain, the U.S. is the hero, the U.S. and other industrialized nations are victims, and the crime is a death threat, that is, a threat to economic health. The American people could not accept the second scenario, since it amounted to trading lives for oil. The administration thus settled on the first scenario, and that seems to have been accepted by the public, the media, and Congress as providing moral justification for going to war.

C. RULER-FOR-STATE METONYMY

There is a metonymy that goes hand-in-hand with the state-as-person metaphor: the ruler stands for the state. Thus we can refer to Iraq by referring to Saddam Hussein, and so have a single person, not just an amorphous state, to play the villain in the just war scenario. It is this metonymy that is invoked when the president says "We have to get Saddam out of Kuwait." Incidentally the metonymy only applies to those leaders perceived as rulers. Thus it would be strange for us, but not for the Iraqis, to describe an American invasion of Kuwait by saying, "George Bush marched into Kuwait."

The Experts' Metaphors

Experts in international relations have an additional system of metaphors that are taken as defining a rational approach. The principal ones are the rational actor metaphor and Clausewitz's metaphor, which are commonly taught as truths in courses on international relations. We are now in a position to show precisely what is metaphorical about Clausewitz's metaphor. To do so we need to look at a system of metaphors that is presupposed by Clausewitz's metaphor. We will begin with an everyday system of metaphors for understanding causation.

A. THE CAUSAL COMMERCE SYSTEM

The causal commerce system is a way to comprehend actions intended to achieve positive effects but which may also have negative effects. The system is composed of three metaphors.

Causal Transfer. An effect is an object transferred from a cause to an affected party. For example sanctions are seen as "giving" Iraq economic difficulties. Correspondingly economic difficulties for Iraq are seen as "coming from" the sanctions. This metaphor turns purposeful actions into transfers of objects.

The Exchange Metaphor for Value. The value of something is what you are willing to exchange for it. Whenever we ask whether it is "worth" going to war to get Iraq out of Kuwait, we are using the exchange metaphor for value plus the causal transfer metaphor.

Well-being is wealth. Things of value constitute wealth. Increases in well-being are "gains," decreases are "costs." The metaphor of well-being as wealth has the effect of making qualitative effects quantitative. It not only makes qualitatively different things comparable, it even provides a kind of calculus for adding up costs and gains. Taken together these three metaphors portray actions as commercial transactions with costs and gains. Seeing action as transactions is crucial to applying ideas from economics to actions in general.

B. RISKS

A risk is an action taken to achieve a positive effect, where the outcome is uncertain and where there is also a significant probability of a negative effect. Since the causal commerce system allows one to see positive effects of actions as "gains" and negative effects as "costs," it becomes natural to see a risky action metaphorically as financial risk of a certain type, namely, a gamble.

Risks as Gambles. In gambling to achieve certain "gains," there are "stakes" that one can "lose." When one asks what is "at stake" in going to war, one is using the metaphors of causal commerce and risks as gambles. These are also the metaphors that President Bush uses when he refers to strategic moves in the gulf as a "poker game" where it would be foolish for him to "show his cards," that is, to make strategic knowledge public.

C. THE MATHEMATICIZATION OF METAPHOR

The causal commerce and risks as gambles metaphors lie behind our everyday way of understanding risky actions as gambles. At this point mathematics enters the picture, since there is a mathematics of gambling, namely probability theory, decision theory, and game theory. Since the metaphors of causal commerce and risks as gambles are so common in our everyday thought, their metaphorical nature often goes unnoticed. As a result it is not uncommon for social scientists to think that the mathematics of gambling literally applies to all forms of risky action, and that it can provide a general basis for the scientific study of risky action, so that risk can be minimized.

D. RATIONAL ACTION

Within the social sciences, especially in economics, it is common to see a rational person as someone who acts in his own self-interest, that is, in order to maximize his own well-being. Hard-core advocates of this view may even see altruistic action as being self-interested if there is a value in feeling righteous about altruism and in deriving gratitude from others. In the causal commerce system, where well-being is wealth, this view of rational action translates metaphorically into maximizing gains and minimizing losses. In other words, in this system:

Rationality is profit maximization.

This metaphor presupposes the causal commerce plus risks as gambles metaphors and brings with it the mathematics of gambling as applied to risky action. It has the effect of turning specialists in mathematical economics into "scientific" specialists in acting rationally so as to minimize risk and cost while maximizing gains.

Suppose we now add the state as person metaphor to the rationality as profit maximization metaphor. The resulting metaphor is:

International Politics is Business.

Here the state is a rational actor, whose actions are transactions and who is engaged in maximizing gains and minimizing costs. This metaphor brings with it the mathematics of cost-benefit calculation and game theory, which is commonly taught in graduate programs in international relations. Clausewitz's metaphor--war is politics pursued by other means--is the major metaphor preferred by international relations strategists and presupposes this system. Since politics is business, war becomes a matter of maximizing political gains and minimizing losses. In Clausewitzian terms war is justified when there is more to be gained by going to war than by not going. Morality is absent from the Clausewitzian equation except when there is a political cost to acting immorally or a political gain from acting morally. Clausewitz's metaphor only allows war to be justified on pragmatic, not moral, grounds. To justify war on both moral and pragmatic grounds, the fairy tale of the just war and Clausewitz's metaphor must mesh. The "worthwhile sacrifices" of the fairy tale must equal the Clausewitzian "costs," and the "victory" in the fairy tale must equal the Clausewitzian "gains." Clausewitz's metaphor is the perfect expert's metaphor, since it requires specialists in political cost-benefit calculation. It sanctions the use of the mathematics of economics, probability theory, decision theory, and game theory in the name of making foreign policy rational and scientific.

Clausewitz's metaphor is commonly seen as literally true. We are now in a position to see exactly what makes it metaphorical. First it uses the state as person metaphor. Second it turns qualitative effects on human beings into quantifiable costs and gains, thus seeing political action as economics. Third it sees rationality as profit making. Fourth it sees war in terms of only one dimension of war, that of political expediency, which is in turn conceptualized as business.

E. WAR AS VIOLENT CRIME

To bear in mind what is hidden by Clausewitz's metaphor, we should consider an alternative metaphor that is not used by professional strategists or by the general public to understand war as we engage in it:

War is Violent Crime--Murder, Assault, Kidnapping, Arson, Rape, and Theft.

In this metaphor war is understood only in terms of its moral dimension and not, say, in its political or economic dimensions. This metaphor highlights those aspects of war that would otherwise be seen as major crimes. There is an us-them asymmetry between the public use of Clausewitz's metaphor and the war as crime metaphor. The Iraqi invasion of Kuwait is reported in terms of murder, theft, and rape, while the planned American invasion is never discussed in terms of murder, assault, and arson. Moreover the U.S. plans for war are seen, in Clausewitzian terms, as rational calculations, but the Iraqi invasion is discussed not as a rational move by Saddam, but as the work of a madman. We see us as rational, moral, and courageous and them as criminal and insane.

F. WAR AS A COMPETITIVE GAME

It has long been noted that we understand war as a competitive game, like chess, or as a sport, like football or boxing. This is a metaphor in which there is a clear winner and loser and a clear end to the game. The metaphor highlights strategic thinking, team work, preparedness, the spectators in the world arena, the glory of winning, and the shame of defeat. This metaphor is taken very seriously. There is a long tradition in the West of training military officers in team sports and chess. The military is trained to win. This can lead to a metaphor conflict, as it did in Vietnam, since Clausewitz's metaphor seeks to maximize geopolitical gains, which may or may not be consistent with absolute military victory. The situation at present is that the public has accepted the rescue scenario of the just war fairy tale as providing moral justification. The president, for internal political reasons, has accepted the competitive game metaphor as taking precedence over Clausewitz's metaphor. If he must choose, he will go for the military win over maximizing geopolitical gains. The testimony of the experts before Congress falls largely within Clausewitz's metaphor. Much of it is testimony about what will maximize gains and minimize losses. For all that has been questioned in the Congressional hearings, these metaphors have not. It is important to see what they hide.

Is Saddam Irrational?

The villain in the fairy tale of the just war may be cunning, but he cannot be rational. You just do not reason with a demon, nor do you enter into negotiations with him. The logic of the metaphor demands that Saddam be irrational. But is he? Administration policy is confused on the issue. Clausewitz's metaphor, as used by strategists, assumes that the enemy is rational; he too is maximizing gains and minimizing costs. Our strategy from the outset has been to "increase the cost" to Saddam. That assumes he is rational and is maximizing his self-interest. At the same time he is being called irrational. The nuclear weapons argument depends on it. If he is rational, he should follow the logic of deterrence. We have thousands of nuclear warheads. Israel is estimated to have between one hundred and two hundred deliverable atomic bombs. It would take Saddam at least eight months and possibly five years before he had a crude, untested atomic bomb on a truck. The most popular estimate for even a few deliverable nuclear warheads is ten years. The argument that he would not be deterred by our nuclear arsenal or by Israel's assumes irrationality.

The Hitler analogy also assumes that Saddam is a villainous madman. The analogy presupposes a Hitler myth, in which Hitler too was an irrational demon, rather than a rational, self-serving brutal politician. In the myth Munich was a mistake and Hitler could have been stopped early on had England entered the war then. Military historians disagree as to whether this myth is true. However, be that as it may, the analogy does not hold. Whether or not Saddam is Hitler, Iraq is not Germany. It has seventeen million people, not seventy. It is economically weak, not strong. It simply is not a threat to the world. Saddam is certainly immoral, ruthless, and brutal, but there is no evidence that he is anything but rational. Everything he has done, from assassinating political opponents, to using poison gas against his political enemies, the Kurds, to invading Kuwait can be seen as furthering his own self-interest.

Kuwait as Victim

The classical victim is innocent. To the Iraqis Kuwait was anything but an innocent ingenue. The war with Iran virtually bankrupted Iraq, which saw itself as having fought that war partly for the benefit of Kuwait and Saudi Arabia, where Shiite citizens supported Khomeini's Islamic revolution. Kuwait had agreed to help finance the war, but afterwards the Kuwaitis insisted on repayment of the "loan." Kuwaitis had invested hundreds of billions of dollars in Europe, America, and Japan, but would not invest in Iraq after the war to help it rebuild. On the contrary Kuwait began what amounted to economic warfare against Iraq by overproducing its oil quota to hold oil prices down. In addition Kuwait drilled laterally into Iraqi territory in the Rumailah oil field and extracted oil from Iraqi territory. Kuwait further took advantage of Iraq by buying its currency, but only at extremely low exchange rates. Subsequently wealthy Kuwaitis used that Iraqi currency on trips to Iraq, where they bought Iraqi goods at bargain rates. Among the things they bought most flamboyantly were liquor and prostitutes--widows and orphans of men killed in the war who, because of the state of the economy, had no other means of support.

All this did not endear Kuwaitis to Iraqis, who were suffering from over 70 percent inflation. Moreover Kuwaitis had long been resented for good reason by Iraqis and Moslems from other nations. Capital rich but labor poor, Kuwait imported cheap labor from other Moslem countries to do its least pleasant work. At the time of the invasion there were 400,000 Kuwaiti citizens and 2.2 million foreign laborers who were denied rights of citizenry and treated by the Kuwaitis as lesser beings. In short, to the Iraqis and to labor-exporting Asian countries, Kuwait is badly miscast as a purely innocent victim. This does not in any way justify the horrors perpetrated on the Kuwaitis by the Iraqi army, but it is part of what is hidden when Kuwait is cast as an innocent victim. The "legitimate government" that we seek to reinstall is an oppressive monarchy.

What is Victory?

In a fairy tale or a game, victory is well defined. Once it is achieved, the story or game is over. Neither is the case in the gulf crisis. History continues, and "victory" makes sense only in terms of continuing history. The president's stated objectives are total Iraqi withdrawal and restoration of the Kuwaiti monarchy. But no one believes the matter will end there, since Saddam would still be in power with all of his forces intact. General Powell said in his Senate testimony that if Saddam withdrew, the U.S. would have to "strengthen the indigenous countries of the region" to achieve a balance of power. Presumably that means arming Assad of Syria, who is every bit as dangerous as Saddam. Would arming another villain count as victory?

If we go to war, what will constitute "victory?" Suppose we conquer Iraq, wiping out its military capability. How would Iraq be governed? No puppet government that we set up could govern effectively, since it would be hated by the entire populace. Since Saddam has wiped out all opposition, the only remaining effective government for the country would be his Ba'ath party. Would it count as a victory if Saddam's friends wound up in power? If not, what other choice is there? And if Iraq has no remaining military force, how could it defend itself against Syria and Iran? It would certainly not be a "victory" for us if either of them took over Iraq. If Syria did, then Assad's Arab nationalism would become a threat; if Iran did, then Islamic fundamentalism would become even more powerful and threatening.

It would seem that the closest thing to a "victory" for the U.S. in case of war would be to drive the Iraqis out of Kuwait; destroy just enough of Iraq's military to leave it capable of defending itself against Syria and Iran; somehow get Saddam out of power but let his Ba'ath party remain in control of a country just strong enough to defend itself, but not strong enough to be a threat; and keep the price of oil at a reasonably low level. The problems: It is not obvious that we could get Saddam out of power without wiping out most of Iraq's military capability. We would have invaded an Arab country, which would create vast hatred for us throughout the Arab world, and would no doubt result in decades of increased terrorism and lack of cooperation by Arab states. By defeating an Arab nationalist state, we would strengthen Islamic fundamentalism. Iraq would remain a cruel dictatorship run by cronies of Saddam. By reinstating the government of Kuwait, we would inflame the hatred of the poor toward the rich throughout the Arab world, and thus increase instability. And the price of oil would go through the roof. Even the closest thing to a victory does not look very victorious. In the debate over whether to go to war, very little time has been spent clarifying what a victory would be. And if "victory" cannot be defined, neither can "worthwhile sacrifice."

The Arab Viewpoint

The metaphors used to conceptualize the gulf crisis hide the most powerful political ideas in the Arab world: Arab nationalism and Islamic fundamentalism. The first seeks to form a racially based all-Arab nation, the second a theocratic all-Islamic state. Though bitterly opposed to one another, they share a great deal. Both are conceptualized in family terms--an Arab brotherhood and an Islamic brotherhood. Both see brotherhoods as more legitimate than existing states. Both are at odds with the state as person metaphor, which sees currently existing states as distinct entities with a right to exist in perpetuity.

Also hidden by our metaphors is perhaps the most important daily concern throughout the Arab world: Arab dignity. Both political movements are seen as ways to achieve dignity though unity. The current national boundaries are widely perceived as working against Arab dignity in two ways, one internal and one external.

The internal issue is the division between rich and poor in the Arab world. Poor Arabs see rich Arabs as rich by accident, by where the British happened to draw the lines that created the contemporary nations of the Middle East. To see Arabs metaphorically as one big family is to suggest that oil wealth should belong to all Arabs. To many Arabs the national boundaries drawn by colonial powers are illegitimate, violating the conception of Arabs as a single "brotherhood" and impoverishing millions. To those impoverished millions, the positive side of Saddam's invasion of Kuwait was that it challenged national borders and brought to the fore the divisions between rich and poor that result from those lines in the sand. If there is to be peace in the region, these divisions must be addressed, say by having rich Arab countries make extensive investments in development that will help poor Arabs. As long as the huge gulf between rich and poor exists in the Arab world, a large number of poor Arabs will continue to see one of the superstate solutions, either Arab nationalism or Islamic fundamentalism, as being in their self-interest, and the region will continue to be unstable.

The external issue is weakness. The current national boundaries keep Arab nations squabbling among themselves and therefore weak relative to Western nations. To unity advocates, what we call "stability" means continued weakness. Weakness is a major theme in the Arab world and is often conceptualized in sexual terms, even more than in the West. American officials, in speaking of the "rape" of Kuwait, are conceptualizing a weak, defenseless country as female and a strong militarily powerful country as male. Similarly it is common for Arabs to conceptualize the colonization and subsequent domination of the Arab world by the West, especially the United States, as emasculation.

An Arab proverb that is reported to be popular in Iraq these days is that "It is better to be a cock for a day than a chicken for a year." The message is clear. It is better to be male, that is, strong and dominant, for a short period than to be female, that is, weak and defenseless, for a long time. Much of the support for Saddam among Arabs is due to the fact that he is seen as standing up to the United States, even if only for a while, and that there is dignity in this.

If upholding dignity is an essential part of what defines Saddam's "rational self-interest," it is vitally important for our government to know this, since he may be willing to go to war to "be a cock for a day." The United States does not have anything like a proper understanding of Arab dignity. Take the question of whether Iraq will come out of this with part of the Rumailah oil fields and two islands giving it a port on the gulf. From Iraq's point of view these are seen as economic necessities if it is to rebuild. President Bush has spoken of this as "rewarding aggression," using the metaphor of Third World countries as children, where the great powers are grownups who have the obligation to reward or punish children so as to make them behave properly. This is exactly the attitude that grates on Arabs who want to be treated with dignity. Instead of seeing Iraq as a sovereign nation that has taken military action for economic purposes, the president treats Iraq as if it were a child gone bad, who has become the neighborhood bully and should be properly disciplined by the grownups. The issue of the Rumailah oil fields and the two islands has alternatively been discussed in the media in terms of "saving face." Saving face is a very different concept from upholding Arab dignity and insisting on being treated as an equal, not an inferior.

What is Hidden By Seeing the State as a Person

The state as person metaphor highlights the ways in which states act as units, and hides the internal structure of the state. Class structure is hidden by this metaphor, as is ethnic composition, religious rivalry, political parties, the ecology, and the influence of the military and of corporations, especially multinational corporations. Consider "national interest." It is in a person's interest to be healthy and strong. The state as person metaphor translates this into a "national interest" of economic health and military strength. But what is in the "national interest" may or may not be in the interest of many ordinary citizens, groups, or institutions, who may become poorer as the GNP rises and weaker as the military gets stronger.

The "national interest" is a metaphorical concept, defined in America by politicians and policy makers. For the most part they are influenced more by the rich than by the poor, more by large corporations than by small businesses, and more by developers than by ecological activists. When President Bush argues that going to war would "serve our vital national interest," he is using a metaphor that hides exactly whose interests would be served and whose would not. For example, poor people, especially blacks and Hispanics, are represented in the military in disproportionately large numbers, and in a war the lower classes and those ethnic groups will suffer proportionally more casualties. Thus war is less in the interest of ethnic minorities and the lower classes than the white upper classes.

Also hidden are the interests of the military itself, which are served when war is justified. Hopes that after the Cold War the military might play a smaller role have been dashed by the president's decision to prepare for war. He was advised, as he should be, by the National Security Council, which consists primarily of military men. War is so awful a prospect that one would not like to think that military self-interest itself could help tilt the balance to a decision for war. But in a democratic society, the question must be asked, since the justifications for war also justify continued military funding and an undiminished national political role for the military.

Energy Policy
The state as person metaphor defines health for the state in economic terms, with our current understanding of economic health taken as a given, including our dependence on foreign oil. Many commentators have argued that a change in energy policy to make us less dependent on foreign oil would be more rational than going to war to preserve our supply of cheap oil from the gulf. This argument may have a real force, but it has no metaphorical force when the definition of economic health is fixed. After all you don't deal with an attack on your health by changing the definition of health. Metaphorical logic pushes a change in energy policy out of the spotlight in the current crisis.

I do not want to give the impression that all that is involved here is metaphor. Obviously there are powerful corporate interests lined up against a fundamental restructuring of our national energy policy. What is sad is that they have a very compelling system of metaphorical thought on their side. If the debate is framed in terms of an attack on our economic health, one cannot argue for redefining what economic health is without changing the grounds of the debate. And if the debate is framed in terms of rescuing a victim, then changes in energy policy seem utterly beside the point.

The "Costs" of War
Clausewitz's metaphor requires a calculation of the "costs" and the "gains" of going to war. What exactly goes into that calculation and what does not? Certainly American casualties, loss of equipment, and dollars spent on the operation count as costs. But Vietnam taught us that there are social costs: trauma to families and communities, disruption of lives, psychological effects on veterans, and long-term health problems, in addition to the cost of spending

our money on war instead of on vital social needs at home. Also hidden are political costs: the enmity of Arabs for many years and the cost of increased terrorism. And barely discussed is the moral cost that comes from killing and maiming as a way to settle disputes. There is the moral cost of using a "cost" metaphor at all. When we do so we quantify the effects of war and thus hide from ourselves the qualitative reality of pain and death. But those are costs to us. What is most ghoulish about the cost-benefit calculation is that "costs" to the other side count as "gains" for us. In Vietnam the body counts of killed Viet Cong were taken as evidence of what was being "gained" in the war. Dead human beings went on the profit side of our ledger. There is a lot of talk of American deaths as "costs," but Iraqi deaths aren't mentioned. The metaphors of cost-benefit accounting and the fairy tale villain lead us to devalue the lives of Iraqis, even when most of those actually killed will not be villains at all, but simply innocent draftees or reservists or civilians.

America as Hero

The classic fairy tale defines what constitutes a hero: it is a person who rescues an innocent victim and who defeats and punishes a guilty and inherently evil villain, and who does so for moral rather than venal reasons. If America starts a war, will it be functioning as a hero? It will certainly not fit the profile very well. First, one of its main goals will be to reinstate "the legitimate government of Kuwait." That means reinstating an absolute monarchy, where women are not accorded anything resembling reasonable rights, and where 80 percent of the people living in the country are foreign workers who do the dirtiest jobs and are not accorded the opportunity to become citizens. This is not an innocent victim whose rescue makes us heroic. Second, the actual human beings who will suffer from an all-out attack will for the most part be innocent people who did not take part in the atrocities in Kuwait. Killing and maiming a lot of innocent bystanders in the process of nabbing a much smaller number of villains does not make one much of a hero. Third, in the self-defense scenario, where oil is at issue, America is acting in its self-interest. But in order to qualify as a legitimate hero in the rescue scenario, it must be acting selflessly. Thus there is a contradiction between the self-interested hero of the self-defense scenario and the purely selfless hero of the rescue scenario. Fourth, America may be a hero to the royal families of Kuwait and Saudi Arabia, but it will not be a hero to most Arabs, who do not think in terms of our metaphors. A great many Arabs will see us as a kind of colonial power using illegitimate force against an Arab brother. To them we will be villains, not heroes.

America appears as a classic hero only if you do not look carefully at how the metaphor is applied to the situation. It is here that the state as person metaphor functions in a way that hides vital truths. The state as person metaphor hides the internal structure of states and allows us to think of Kuwait as a unitary entity, the defenseless maiden to be rescued in the fairy tale. The metaphor hides the monarchical character of Kuwait and the way Kuwaitis treat women and the vast majority of the people who live in their country. The state as person metaphor also hides the internal structures of Iraq, and thus hides the actual people who will be killed, maimed, or otherwise harmed in a war. The same metaphor also hides the internal poor and minorities who will make the most sacrifices while not getting any significant benefit. And it hides the main ideas that drive Middle Eastern politics.

Things to Do

War would create much more suffering than it would alleviate, and should be renounced in this case on humanitarian grounds. There is no shortage of alternatives to war. Troops can be rotated out and brought to the minimum level to deter an invasion of Saudi Arabia. Economic sanctions can be continued. A serious system of international inspections can be instituted to prevent the development of Iraq's nuclear capacity. A certain amount of "face-saving" for Saddam is better than war. As part of a compromise the Kuwaiti monarchy can be sacrificed and elections held in Kuwait. The problems of rich and poor Arabs must be addressed, with pressures placed on the Kuwaitis and others to invest significantly in development to help poor Arabs. Balance of power solutions within the region should always be seen as moves toward reducing, not increasing armaments; positive economic incentives can be used, together with the threat of refusal by us and the Soviets to supply spare parts needed to keep hi-tech military weaponry functional. If there is a moral to come out of the Congressional hearings, it is that there are a lot of very knowledgeable people in this country who have thought about alternatives to war. They should be taken seriously.

CONTRIBUTORS

BRIEN HALLETT teaches English at the University of Hawai'i at Mānoa and is a council member of the Matsunaga Institute for Peace.

MEREDITH L. KILGORE is a graduate student in political student at the University of Hawai'i at Mānoa.

GEORGE LAKOFF is a professor of linguistics at the University of California at Berkeley. In addition to numerous works on structural linguistics, he is the author of several studies on metaphor, including *Metaphors We Live By* (with Mark Johnson), *More Than Cool Reason: A Field Guide to Poetic Metaphor* (with Mark Turner), and *Women, Fire and Dangerous Things: What Categories Reveal About the Mind.*

DONALD A. WELLS is professor emeritus of philosophy at the University of Hawai'i at Hilo. He followed the release of the second edition of his *War Crimes and Laws of War* with a nationwide lecture tour examining the gulf war from the perspective of the just war tradition.

ROGER WILLIAMSON is a researcher with the Life and Peace Institute in Uppsala, Sweden. He lives in London and is the author of numerous studies on ecumenical social ethics and peace research.

Publications of the Matsunaga Institute for Peace

The Matsunaga Institute for Peace publishes scholarly and creative works on peace in all media. The publications are available from the institute (Matsunaga Institute for Peace, University of Hawai'i, Porteus Hall 717, 2424 Maile Way, Honolulu, Hawai'i, USA 96822; 808-956-7718, FAX 808-956-5708).

Solving Conflicts: A Peace Research Perspective, by Johan Galtung. In conjunction with the University of Hawaii Press. 1989. 62 pp. $8.

Peace and Development in the Pacific, by Johan Galtung. In conjunction with the University of Hawaii Press. 1989. 68 pp. $8.

Nonviolence and Israel/Palestine, by Johan Galtung. In conjunction with the University of Hawaii Press. 1989. 79 pp. $10.

Peace Studies: The Evolution of Peace Research and Peace Education, by Carolyn Stephenson. Occasional Paper 1. 1990. 19 pp. $2.

War and Children's Survival, by George Kent. Occasional Paper 2. 1990. 33 pp. $2.

Letters from Jerusalem, edited by Majid Tehranian. Occasional Paper 4. 1990. 87 pp. $4.

Restructuring for Ethnic Peace: A Public Debate at the University of Hawai'i, edited by Majid Tehranian. 187 pp. Fall 1991.

Implementing the Rights of Children in Armed Conflict, by George Kent. Working Paper 1. 20 pp. Fall 1991.

In addition, the Institute distributes the following publications from the Center for Global Nonviolence Planning Project of the University of Hawai'i:

Nonviolence and Hawaii's Spiritual Traditions, edited by Glenn D. Paige and Sarah Gilliatt. 1991. 103 pp. $5.

Buddhism and Nonviolent Global Problem-Solving, edited by Glenn D. Paige and Sarah Gilliatt. 1991. 176 pp. $10.

INDEX